Editorial Development: Marilyn Evans
Robyn Raymer
Sarita Chávez
Silverman
Stephanie Wright
Copy Editing: Carrie Gwynne
Art Direction: Cheryl Puckett
Cover Design: David Price
Design/Production: Susan Bigger
John D. Williams

EMC 2796

Evan-Moor
EDUCATIONAL PUBLISHERS®
Helping Children Learn since 1979

Congratulations on your purchase of some of the finest teaching materials in the world.

Photocopying the pages in this book is permitted for <u>single-classroom use only</u>. Making photocopies for additional classes or schools is prohibited.

For information about other Evan-Moor products, call 1-800-777-4362, fax 1-800-777-4332, or visit our Web site, www.evan-moor.com. Entire contents © 2009 EVAN-MOOR CORP. 18 Lower Ragsdale Drive, Monterey, CA 93940-5746. Printed in USA.

Correlated
to State Standards

Visit *teaching-standards.com* to view a correlation of this book's activities to your state's standards. This is a free service.

Weekly Walk-Through

Each week of **A Word a Day** follows the same format, making it easy for both students and teacher to use.

Words of the Week

Four new words are presented each week. A definition, example sentence, and discussion prompts are provided for each word.

Part of Speech The part of speech is identified. You may or may not want to share this information with the class, depending on the skill level of your students.

Example Sentence Each new word is used in a sentence designed to provide enough context for students to easily grasp its meaning. The same sentence is found in the reproducible student dictionary, which begins on page 148.

Critical Attributes Prompt Discussion questions are provided that require students to identify features that are and are not attributes of the target word. This is one of the most effective ways to help students recognize subtleties of meaning.

Definition Each word is defined. The same definition is found in the reproducible student dictionary, which begins on page 148.

Graphic Organizer Prompt One word each week requires completion of a graphic organizer.

Personal Connection Prompt Students are asked to share an opinion, an idea, or a personal experience that demonstrates their understanding of the new word.

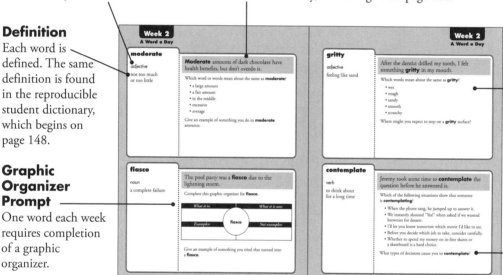

How to Present the Words

Use one of the following methods to present each word:

- Write the word on the board. Then read the definition and the example sentence, explaining as needed before conducting oral activities.

- Make an overhead transparency of the lesson page that shows the word. Then guide students through the definition, example sentence, and oral activities. Make a transparency of page 159 to use with lessons that feature a graphic organizer.

- Reproduce the dictionary on pages 148–158 for each student, or provide each student with a student practice book. (See inside front cover.) Have students find the word in their dictionary and then guide them through the definition, example sentence, and oral activities.

End-of-Week Review

Review the four words of the week through oral and written activities designed to reinforce student understanding.

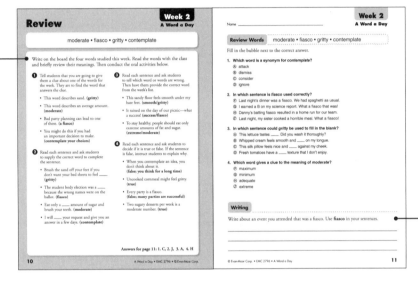

Oral Review
Four oral activities provide you with prompts to review the week's words.

Written Assessment
A student reproducible containing four multiple-choice items and an open-ended writing activity can be used to assess students' mastery.

Additional Features

- Reproducible student dictionary

- Cumulative word index

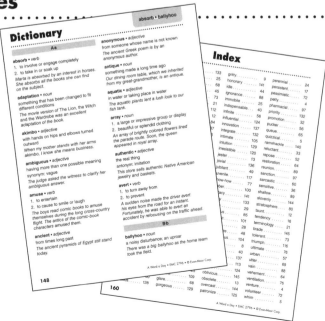

petty

adjective

not important

When we divided the lunch bill, it seemed **petty** to argue over who would pay the extra five cents.

Complete this graphic organizer for **petty**.

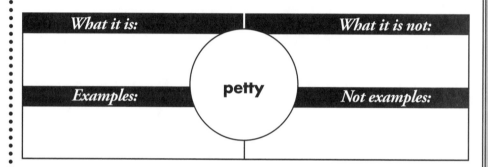

What it is:		*What it is not:*
	petty	
Examples:		*Not examples:*

What are some other things that you think are too **petty** to argue about?

venture

noun

a risky or uncertain undertaking

The business **venture** turned out to be a financial disaster.

Which of these are **ventures**?

- a guaranteed success
- a bet
- an adventure into the unknown
- a sure thing
- a chance

Are there any **ventures** you might like to be involved in? What are they? Why would you be willing to take the risk?

whim

noun

a sudden idea to do something

> I'd planned to clean out my closet today, but on a **whim**, I decided to go roller-skating.

Which of the following show acting on a **whim**?

- We have been planning our trip to Italy for a year.
- Grandpa put down his newspaper and announced that we were all going out for ice cream.
- It was such a nice day that we went to the beach instead of the movies.
- He practices the trumpet daily and hopes to be chosen for the high school jazz band.
- I love that song. Let's dance!

What are some things you sometimes do on a **whim**?

quizzical

adjective

expressing doubt or questioning; puzzled

> Mom looked **quizzical** when she received a birthday card from someone whose name she didn't recognize.

Which words mean about the same as **quizzical**?

- perplexed
- certain
- convinced
- confused
- befuddled

How would you look if you were **quizzical**? Try it.

Review

petty • venture • whim • quizzical

Write on the board the four words studied this week. Read the words with the class and briefly review their meanings. Then conduct the oral activities below.

1 Tell students that you are going to give them a clue about one of the words for the week. They are to find the word that answers the clue.

- This word describes what it is like to argue over silly details. **(petty)**

- You might look this way if you didn't understand something. **(quizzical)**

- This word describes an undertaking with an uncertain result. **(a venture)**

- One of these may cause you to do something unplanned. **(a whim)**

2 Read each sentence and ask students to supply the correct word to complete the sentence.

- Mr. Pine invested money in his sister's business ____. **(venture)**

- On a ____, Mom decided we'd go to a restaurant instead of eating dinner at home. **(whim)**

- Your ____ expression tells me my explanation didn't make sense. **(quizzical)**

- These details are important, not ____. **(petty)**

3 Read each sentence and ask students to tell which word or words are wrong. Then have them provide the correct word from the week's list.

- When Taylor feels confused, she looks certain. **(certain/quizzical)**

- It's very important to figure out exactly how many pennies you owe me. **(very important/petty)**

- Suddenly, a carefully planned idea came to me: I'd phone and ask if Shelby wanted to go to the park. **(carefully planned idea/whim)**

4 Read each sentence and ask students to decide if it is true or false. If the sentence is false, instruct students to explain why.

- To do something on a whim, you plan it in advance. **(false; a whim comes to you suddenly)**

- You can't be sure that a venture will succeed. **(true)**

- Petty details aren't worth arguing over. **(true)**

- People may look quizzical when something puzzles them. **(true)**

Answers for page 7: 1. A, 2. J, 3. A, 4. G

| Review Words | petty • venture • whim • quizzical |

Fill in the bubble next to the correct answer.

1. Which word is a synonym for *quizzical*?

Ⓐ puzzled

Ⓑ mental

Ⓒ certain

Ⓓ furious

2. In which sentence is *whim* used correctly?

Ⓕ What is the solution to this whim?

Ⓖ After weeks of planning, I formed a whim.

Ⓗ I think this room needs another whim.

Ⓙ On a whim, we had popcorn for dinner.

3. In which sentence could *petty* be used fill in the blank?

Ⓐ Don't waste time on _____ concerns.

Ⓑ A _____ disaster occurred last summer.

Ⓒ Amy wore a _____ outfit to school today.

Ⓓ If you are _____ today, you'll receive a reward.

4. Which word gives a clue to the meaning of *venture*?

Ⓕ excellent

Ⓖ uncertain

Ⓗ protective

Ⓙ conceited

| Writing |

Write about something that people should not do "on a whim." Use **whim** in your sentences.

_____

_____

_____

moderate

adjective

not too much
or too little

Moderate amounts of dark chocolate have health benefits, but don't overdo it.

Which word or words mean about the same as **moderate**?

- a large amount
- a fair amount
- in the middle
- excessive
- average

Give an example of something you do in **moderate** amounts.

fiasco

noun

a complete failure

The pool party was a **fiasco** due to the lightning storm.

Complete this graphic organizer for **fiasco**.

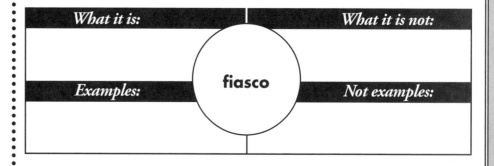

Give an example of something you tried that turned into a **fiasco**.

gritty

adjective

feeling like sand

After the dentist drilled my tooth, I felt something **gritty** in my mouth.

Which words mean about the same as **gritty**?

- wet
- rough
- sandy
- smooth
- scratchy

Where might you expect to step on a **gritty** surface?

contemplate

verb

to think about for a long time

Jeremy took some time to **contemplate** the question before he answered it.

Which of the following situations show that someone is **contemplating**?

- When the phone rang, he jumped up to answer it.
- We instantly shouted "Yes!" when asked if we wanted brownies for dessert.
- I'll let you know tomorrow which movie I'd like to see.
- Before you decide which job to take, consider carefully.
- Whether to spend my money on in-line skates or a skateboard is a hard choice.

What types of decisions cause you to **contemplate**?

Review

moderate • fiasco • gritty • contemplate

Write on the board the four words studied this week. Read the words with the class and briefly review their meanings. Then conduct the oral activities below.

1 Tell students that you are going to give them a clue about one of the words for the week. They are to find the word that answers the clue.

- This word describes sand. **(gritty)**

- This word describes an average amount. **(moderate)**

- Bad party planning can lead to one of these. **(a fiasco)**

- You might do this if you had an important decision to make. **(contemplate your choices)**

2 Read each sentence and ask students to supply the correct word to complete the sentence.

- Brush the sand off your feet if you don't want your bed sheets to feel ____. **(gritty)**

- The student body election was a ____ because the wrong names were on the ballot. **(fiasco)**

- Eat only a ____ amount of sugar and brush your teeth. **(moderate)**

- I will ____ your request and give you an answer in a few days. **(contemplate)**

3 Read each sentence and ask students to tell which word or words are wrong. Then have them provide the correct word from the week's list.

- This sandy floor feels smooth under my bare feet. **(smooth/gritty)**

- It rained on the day of our picnic—what a success! **(success/fiasco)**

- To stay healthy, people should eat only extreme amounts of fat and sugar. **(extreme/moderate)**

4 Read each sentence and ask students to decide if it is true or false. If the sentence is false, instruct students to explain why.

- When you contemplate an idea, you don't think about it. **(false; you think for a long time)**

- Uncooked cornmeal might feel gritty. **(true)**

- Every party is a fiasco. **(false; many parties are successful)**

- Two sugary desserts per week is a moderate number. **(true)**

Answers for page 11: 1. C, 2. J, 3. A, 4. H

| **Review Words** | moderate • fiasco • gritty • contemplate |

Fill in the bubble next to the correct answer.

1. **Which word is a synonym for *contemplate*?**
   Ⓐ attack
   Ⓑ dismiss
   Ⓒ consider
   Ⓓ ignore

2. **In which sentence is *fiasco* used correctly?**
   Ⓕ Last night's dinner was a fiasco. We had spaghetti as usual.
   Ⓖ I earned a B on my science report. What a fiasco that was!
   Ⓗ Danny's batting fiasco resulted in a home run for our team.
   Ⓙ Last night, my sister cooked a horrible meal. What a fiasco!

3. **In which sentence could *gritty* be used to fill in the blank?**
   Ⓐ This lettuce tastes ____. Did you wash it thoroughly?
   Ⓑ Whipped cream feels smooth and ____ on my tongue.
   Ⓒ This silk pillow feels nice and ____ against my cheek.
   Ⓓ Fresh tomatoes have a ____ texture that I don't enjoy.

4. **Which word gives a clue to the meaning of *moderate*?**
   Ⓕ maximum
   Ⓖ minimum
   Ⓗ adequate
   Ⓙ extreme

Writing

Write about an event you attended that was a fiasco. Use **fiasco** in your sentences.

_____

_____

_____

diplomatic

adjective

skillful at dealing with people

My teacher is so **diplomatic** at giving feedback that I never get my feelings hurt when she corrects me.

Which of the following people most need to be **diplomatic**?

- a political leader
- a sanitation worker
- an attorney
- a principal
- a baby

Describe someone you know who is **diplomatic**.

taunt

verb

to tease or make fun of

synonym: mock

The zookeeper had to reprimand some teenagers who were **taunting** the lion by poking sticks through the bars of its cage.

Which words mean about the same as **taunt**?

- jeer at
- help
- tantalize
- praise
- ridicule

How would you deal with someone who is **taunting** you?

jester

noun

someone who always jokes or acts playfully

Always the **jester**, Billy showed up for the field trip wearing his sister's bunny slippers.

Which entertainers could be called **jesters**?

- comedians
- rock stars
- acrobats
- singers
- clowns

Do you know anyone who is a **jester**? Is this person fun to be around? Why?

obsolete

adjective

no longer in use

Just as CDs made records a thing of the past, DVDs made videocassettes **obsolete**.

Complete this graphic organizer for **obsolete**.

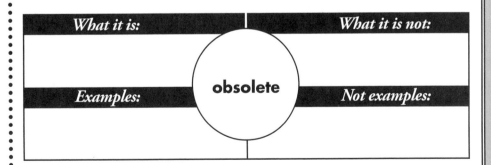

What it is:		*What it is not:*
	obsolete	
Examples:		*Not examples:*

Name some other objects that have become **obsolete**. Why did they become **obsolete**?

Review

diplomatic • taunt • jester • obsolete

Write on the board the four words studied this week. Read the words with the class and briefly review their meanings. Then conduct the oral activities below.

1 Tell students that you are going to give them a clue about one of the words for the week. They are to find the word that answers the clue.

- This word describes turntables on which people used to play vinyl records. **(obsolete)**

- This word describes someone who can get people to work together. **(diplomatic)**

- It is cruel to do this to others. **(taunt them)**

- A person who is a cutup could also be called this. **(a jester)**

2 Read each sentence and ask students to supply the correct word to complete the sentence.

- Ronnie is a ____ who keeps us in stitches with his silly faces. **(jester)**

- A good leader is ____ enough to get along with various groups and individuals. **(diplomatic)**

- The flat screen will make other types of TV and computer screens ____. **(obsolete)**

- Bullies often ____ younger children by calling them names. **(taunt)**

3 Read each sentence and ask students to tell which word or words are wrong. Then have them provide the correct word from the week's list.

- It is insulting to listen carefully when others are speaking. **(insulting/diplomatic)**

- Don't cheer for other people. It is a very mean thing to do. **(cheer for/taunt)**

- Today, the VCR is a state-of-the-art device. **(a state-of-the-art/an obsolete)**

4 Read each sentence and ask students to decide if it is true or false. If the sentence is false, instruct students to explain why.

- You might call the clowns at a circus jesters. **(true)**

- Gas-powered cars are obsolete. **(false; we still use them)**

- *Taunt* and *jeer* are synonyms. **(true)**

- *Diplomatic* and *rude* are antonyms. **(true)**

Answers for page 15: 1. A, 2. G, 3. A, 4. J

Review Words	diplomatic • taunt • jester • obsolete

Fill in the bubble next to the correct answer.

1. **Which phrase means the opposite of *obsolete*?**
   - Ⓐ state of the art
   - Ⓑ old-fashioned
   - Ⓒ over the hill
   - Ⓓ out of circulation

2. **In which sentence is *diplomatic* used correctly?**
   - Ⓕ Daryl is so diplomatic that she can't help insulting people.
   - Ⓖ Danny is diplomatic enough to avoid conflicts with others.
   - Ⓗ Too diplomatic to wait, the children burst into the room.
   - Ⓙ Our diplomatic dog pushes the cats aside and eats their food.

3. **In which sentence could *jester* be used to fill in the blank?**
   - Ⓐ The party was a lot more fun because Candace assumed the role of ____.
   - Ⓑ The bank ____ carefully counted out Molly's money.
   - Ⓒ At the supermarket, I saw a ____ stacking soup cans.
   - Ⓓ The ____ galloped the racehorse across the finish line.

4. **Which word is a synonym for *taunt*?**
   - Ⓕ praise
   - Ⓖ assist
   - Ⓗ confuse
   - Ⓙ mock

Writing

Write about a device or product that you think will soon become obsolete. Explain why. Use **obsolete** in your sentences.

_____

_____

exaggerate

verb

to make something seem larger, more important, or more valuable than it actually is

Tall tales usually **exaggerate** and attribute superhuman traits to the characters.

Complete this graphic organizer for **exaggerate**.

Examples:

exaggerate

Other Ways to Say It:

Tell about a time when you **exaggerated** to make something more interesting or humorous.

tendency

noun

a likelihood of behaving in a certain way

A puppy has a **tendency** to chew on things.

Which of these describe a **tendency**?

- a pattern of doing something
- a predictable behavior
- an unexpected event
- a complete surprise
- a sure bet

What do you have a **tendency** to do?

persistent

adjective

1. not giving up
2. lasting a long time

The **persistent** hikers finally overcame the last obstacle and reached the summit. Their ordeal left them with **persistent** aches and pains.

Which definition is being used: "not giving up" or "lasting a long time"?

- The persistent runner was determined to break the world record for the mile.
- The teacher gave Ana a lecture for her persistent talking.
- The persistent salesperson wouldn't take no for an answer.
- Jane's parents worried about her persistent cough.
- One must be persistent to learn to play an instrument.

When is it a good idea to be **persistent**? When might it be more effective to be flexible rather than **persistent**?

extricate

verb

to set free from a difficult or embarrassing situation

antonym: to trap

The bear struggled to **extricate** itself from the net.

Which of these actions might you perform in order to **extricate** something?

- untie
- unlock
- capture
- release
- enclose

Describe a time when you had to **extricate** yourself or someone else from an uncomfortable situation. Where were you, and how did you **extricate** yourself or the person?

exaggerate • tendency • persistent • extricate

Write on the board the four words studied this week. Read the words with the class and briefly review their meanings. Then conduct the oral activities below.

1 Tell students that you are going to give them a clue about one of the words for the week. They are to find the word that answers the clue.

- You do this when you complain that someone has told you something a hundred times. (**exaggerate**)

- This word describes a cold that lasts for weeks. (**persistent**)

- If a fly got caught in a spider's web, it probably couldn't do this. (**extricate itself**)

- This is someone's habit of behaving a certain way. (**a tendency**)

2 Read each sentence and ask students to supply the correct word to complete the sentence.

- Mom has a ____ to complain about the weather. (**tendency**)

- Don't ____! I have not told that story fifty times! (**exaggerate**)

- If you are ____, you can finish the job by Monday. (**persistent**)

- I was unable to ____ myself from my promise to help weed the garden. (**extricate**)

3 Read each sentence and ask students to tell which word or words are wrong. Then have them provide the correct word from the week's list.

- The dolphin tried to tangle itself in the fishing net. (**tangle itself in/extricate itself from**)

- I had a short illness that lasted for a month. (**short/persistent**)

- Please don't minimize this minor incident. It was not a big deal at all. (**minimize/exaggerate**)

4 Read each sentence and ask students to decide if it is true or false. If the sentence is false, instruct students to explain why.

- Many people have a tendency to gossip about others. (**true**)

- It is impossible for a fish to extricate itself from a fishhook. (**false; fish sometimes free themselves from hooks**)

- *Persistent* and *lackadaisical* are antonyms. (**true**)

- *Exaggerate* and *underestimate* are antonyms. (**true**)

Answers for page 19: 1. D, 2. G, 3. A, 4. H

| Review Words | exaggerate • tendency • persistent • extricate |

Fill in the bubble next to the correct answer.

1. **Which word is a synonym for *extricate*?**
   Ⓐ divide
   Ⓑ contain
   Ⓒ imprison
   Ⓓ disentangle

2. **In which sentence is *persistent* used correctly?**
   Ⓕ Amy is so persistent that she rarely finishes her homework.
   Ⓖ Anna is persistent enough to work on a project until it is done.
   Ⓗ Stop being so persistent. Look on the bright side of situations.
   Ⓙ Our persistent dog refuses to go outside unless we come, too.

3. **In which sentence could *tendency* be used to fill in the blank?**
   Ⓐ Alexa has an annoying ____ to show up late to events.
   Ⓑ I have a great ____ for sweet desserts such as ice cream.
   Ⓒ Aaron has an amazing ____ in math skills.
   Ⓓ Which ____ of Allison's is most expensive and beautiful?

4. **Which sentence illustrates the meaning of *exaggerate*?**
   Ⓕ I've told you twice to stop taunting your sister!
   Ⓖ That is the biggest ice-cream sundae I've ever seen!
   Ⓗ There were about a million people in line for the movie!
   Ⓙ I bet I have at least five pairs of tennis shoes in my closet.

| Writing |

Write about something you want badly enough to be persistent in your plan to get it. Use **persistent** in your sentences.

_____

_____

frontier

noun

the farthest reaches
of settlement,
exploration,
or knowledge

There are few geographic **frontiers** remaining on Earth, but science has many new **frontiers** to explore.

In which of the following is a **frontier** being described?

- The space mission was to explore beyond the solar system.
- Yellowstone is a national park in Wyoming.
- The researcher was trying to find a cure for diabetes.
- That portion of Antarctica is unexplored.
- Perhaps someday, computers will actually think.

What do you think some new **frontiers** in science may be in the twenty-first century?

flaunt

verb

to display noticeably

My cousin loves to **flaunt** her expensive clothes whenever she has a chance.

Which word or words mean about the same as **flaunt**?

- parade around
- show off
- cover up
- exhibit
- hide

Tell about something you like to **flaunt**.

terminology

noun

the special vocabulary used in a particular business, science, or art

synonym: lingo

Words like *byte, software,* and *operating system* are examples of computer **terminology**.

Complete this graphic organizer for **terminology**.

Examples:

terminology

Other Ways to Say It:

Can you give examples of the **terminology** used in another field of science?

digit

noun

1. a numeral
2. a finger or toe

How many **digits** are in the number *one million*? Do you have enough **digits** to represent all those zeros?

Which definition is being used: "a numeral" or "a finger"?

- Ralph is teaching his cousin how to count to ten on her digits.
- Can you tell me what digit is in the tens place?
- I rushed to the emergency room after the door slammed on my middle digit!
- I can't read the digits on my calculator, because the sun is too bright!

Which animals have **digits** similar to a human's?

frontier • flaunt • terminology • digit

Write on the board the four words studied this week. Read the words with the class and briefly review their meanings. Then conduct the oral activities below.

1 Tell students that you are going to give them a clue about one of the words for the week. They are to find the word that answers the clue.

- Six (6) is one. (**a digit**)

- This is a synonym for *lingo*. (**terminology**)

- In the 1800s, many North American settlers traveled west to get there. (**the frontier**)

- You do this if you have new clothes that you want everyone to see. (**flaunt them**)

2 Read each sentence and ask students to supply the correct word to complete the sentence.

- If you want your talents to be recognized, it may be necessary to ____ them. (**flaunt**)

- Developing cancer treatments is an important modern medical ____. (**frontier**)

- Your thumb is a ____, and so is your pinkie finger. (**digit**)

- Cooking ____ includes words such as *dice* and *season*. (**terminology**)

3 Read each sentence and ask students to tell which word or words are wrong. Then have them provide the correct word from the week's list.

- In the 1800s, North American settlers traveled to the big city in wagon trains. (**big city/frontier**)

- Marty is so proud of her artistic talent that she hides her drawing skills. (**hides/flaunts**)

- In one million and one (1,000,001), which letter is in the tens place? (**letter/digit**)

4 Read each sentence and ask students to decide if it is true or false. If the sentence is false, instruct students to explain why.

- The words *virus* and *mouse* are examples of computer terminology. (**true**)

- A person has ten digits on each hand. (**false; he or she has five**)

- Los Angeles is a frontier. (**false; people settled there long ago**)

- *Flaunt* and *display* are synonyms. (**true**)

Answers for page 23: 1. A, 2. G, 3. A, 4. G

| **Review Words** | frontier • flaunt • terminology • digit |

Fill in the bubble next to the correct answer.

1. **Which word is a synonym for *digit*?**
   - Ⓐ finger
   - Ⓑ hand
   - Ⓒ foot
   - Ⓓ leg

2. **In which sentence is *terminology* used correctly?**
   - Ⓕ Don't use that terminology in class, or the principal may suspend you.
   - Ⓖ I don't know much computer terminology, except words like "download."
   - Ⓗ English terminology includes French words such as "cafe" and "chic."
   - Ⓙ I find Alma's terminology hard to understand because she mumbles.

3. **In which sentence could *frontier* be used to fill in the blank?**
   - Ⓐ People often say that space is "the final ____."
   - Ⓑ We'll travel to the ____ next weekend and stay in a motel.
   - Ⓒ In Yosemite National Park, we hiked up a steep, lofty ____.
   - Ⓓ I've never visited New York, but a ____ of mine is going there.

4. **Which word is an antonym for *flaunt*?**
   - Ⓕ reveal
   - Ⓖ conceal
   - Ⓗ criticize
   - Ⓙ praise

| **Writing** |

Write about someone you know who flaunts his or her skills, talents, or possessions.
Use **flaunt** in your sentences.

_____

_____

_____

perennial

adjective

lasting through the year or for many years

synonym: constant

Perennial flowers, such as roses and irises, are sure to bloom again next year.

Which words mean about the same as **perennial**?

- seasonal
- temporary
- everlasting
- year-round
- permanent

What kinds of **perennial** plants can you name?

comprehend

verb

to understand

A good teacher can help you **comprehend** even difficult math problems.

Which words mean about the same as **comprehend**?

- misinterpret
- realize
- grasp
- get
- know

Are there any subjects that were once difficult for you to understand, but now are easy to **comprehend**?

deception

noun

a trick or lie meant
to deceive someone

The movie villain's **deception** to disguise his
identity was uncovered by the clever detective.

Which words mean about the same as **deception**?

- dishonesty
- honesty
- hoax
- fraud
- truth

Tell about a time when you used **deception** to get what you
wanted. Do you think using **deception** is a good idea?

immobile

adjective

unable to move

synonym:
motionless

A car is totally **immobile** without its battery.

Complete this graphic organizer for **immobile**.

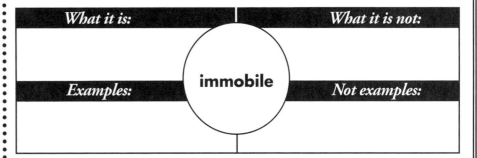

How would you feel if you had to remain completely
immobile for a long time?

Review

perennial • comprehend • deception • immobile

Write on the board the four words studied this week. Read the words with the class and briefly review their meanings. Then conduct the oral activities below.

1 Tell students that you are going to give them a clue about one of the words for the week. They are to find the word that answers the clue.

- Lying is one example of this. (**deception**)

- This word describes a plant that lives for many years. (**perennial**)

- If a kindergartner tried to read a book for young adults, he or she probably couldn't do this. (**comprehend it**)

- This word describes someone who is "paralyzed with fear." (**immobile**)

2 Read each sentence and ask students to supply the correct word to complete the sentence.

- Terrified by the car's headlights, the deer stood ____ by the roadside. (**immobile**)

- Magicians practice ____ when they do tricks. (**deception**)

- Each year, this ____ bush produces beautiful flowers. (**perennial**)

- At first, I didn't ____ the movie's complicated plot. (**comprehend**)

3 Read each sentence and ask students to tell which word is wrong. Then have them provide the correct word from the week's list.

- Spies are noted for their honesty. (**honesty/deception**)

- I can't misunderstand the algebra problems in my older brother's math book. (**misunderstand/comprehend**)

- Amazed, Rachel stood there as jumpy as a statue. (**jumpy/immobile**)

- By next year, this annual bush will have grown at least a foot. (**annual/ perennial**)

4 Read each sentence and ask students to decide if it is true or false. If the sentence is false, instruct students to explain why.

- A perennial plant dies in autumn. (**false; it may live for many years**)

- Most statues are immobile. (**true**)

- A successful surprise party may require deception. (**true**)

- *Comprehend* and *misinterpret* are antonyms. (**true**)

Answers for page 27: 1. C, 2. G, 3. B, 4. J

Review Words perennial • comprehend • deception • immobile

Fill in the bubble next to the correct answer.

1. **Which word is a synonym for *comprehend*?**
   - Ⓐ instruct
   - Ⓑ write
   - Ⓒ understand
   - Ⓓ read

2. **In which sentence is *perennial* used correctly?**
   - Ⓕ This perennial plant blooms in the summertime and dies in the fall.
   - Ⓖ A rosebush is a perennial plant that can live for many, many years.
   - Ⓗ Emma has a perennial habit of biting her fingernails occasionally.
   - Ⓙ Try to be perennial and look at the problem from a new perspective.

3. **Which is an example of *deception*?**
   - Ⓐ explaining a difficult math problem to a family member
   - Ⓑ lying about your true reason for turning down an invitation
   - Ⓒ failing to follow a recipe because you prefer to cook creatively
   - Ⓓ revealing a secret to a good friend because you trust him or her

4. **Which word is an antonym for *immobile*?**
   - Ⓕ motionless
   - Ⓖ wispy
   - Ⓗ beautiful
   - Ⓙ fidgety

Writing

Write about something you had to work hard to comprehend. Use **comprehend** in your sentences.

_____

_____

_____

avert

verb

1. to turn away from
2. to prevent

A sudden noise made the driver **avert** his eyes from the road for an instant. Fortunately, he was able to **avert** an accident by refocusing on the traffic ahead.

Which definition is being used: "to turn away from" or "to prevent"?

- In some cultures, children avert their eyes when speaking to adults.
- She averted her eyes from the horror movie.
- The drivers were able to avert the accident by swerving.
- To avert a fire, never leave home with the iron turned on.
- The teacher tried to avert the class's attention from the scuffle on the playground.

Do you participate in any activities in which you need to be careful to **avert** serious injuries?

majority

noun

more than half or most of something

The **majority** of the students in my class ride a bus to school. The **majority** opinion is that riding the bus is fun.

Which of these mean about the same as **majority**?

- the greater number
- the most popular
- the largest part
- only a few
- a little bit

What does the **majority** of your class like to do at recess?

fastidious

adjective

not easy to please

The **fastidious** eater complained about every dish served at dinner.

Complete this graphic organizer for **fastidious**.

What it is:		*What it is not:*
	fastidious	
Examples:		*Not examples:*

Who is the most **fastidious** person you know?

lunge

verb

to move forward suddenly

The kitten **lunged** at my fish sandwich.

Which of these mean about the same as **lunge**?

- to come after someone
- to jump toward
- to lean back
- to sit down
- to attack

Tell about a time when someone or something **lunged** at you. Where were you and what happened?

avert • majority • fastidious • lunge

Write on the board the four words studied this week. Read the words with the class and briefly review their meanings. Then conduct the oral activities below.

1 Tell students that you are going to give them a clue about one of the words for the week. They are to find the word that answers the clue.

- Ball players sometimes have to do this to catch balls. **(lunge)**

- This word describes someone who's very picky. **(fastidious)**

- Fifteen out of twenty people is one. **(a majority)**

- You do this when you take steps to prevent an accident. **(avert it)**

2 Read each sentence and ask students to supply the correct word to complete the sentence.

- Don't be so ____. How do you know you won't like this dish unless you try it? **(fastidious)**

- When rattlesnakes strike, they ____ at their prey. **(lunge)**

- Please ____ your eyes from my computer screen while I read this private e-mail. **(avert)**

- If a ____ of voters vote for our candidate, she will win the election. **(majority)**

3 Read each sentence and ask students to tell which word or words are wrong. Then have them provide the correct word from the week's list.

- In a democracy, the minority rules. **(minority/majority)**

- A lion may hide in the tall grass and jump away from a passing antelope. **(jump away from/lunge at)**

- Aimee is so easygoing that she is almost impossible to please. **(easygoing/fastidious)**

- Taking every safety precaution may cause an accident. **(cause/avert)**

4 Read each sentence and ask students to decide if it is true or false. If the sentence is false, instruct students to explain why.

- A majority is half of a whole. **(false; it is more than half)**

- *Lunge* and *pounce* have almost the same meaning. **(true)**

- It is difficult to cook for a fastidious person. **(true)**

- *Avert* and *trigger* are antonyms. **(true)**

Answers for page 31: 1. C, 2. F, 3. C, 4. H

| **Review Words** | avert • majority • fastidious • lunge |

Fill in the bubble next to the correct answer.

1. **Which word is an antonym for *majority*?**
   - Ⓐ particle
   - Ⓑ whole
   - Ⓒ minority
   - Ⓓ portion

2. **In which sentence is *avert* used correctly?**
   - Ⓕ I plug my ears and avert my eyes during scary scenes in movies.
   - Ⓖ You have to avert your eyes to see the tiny print on this page.
   - Ⓗ Avert your eyes over there, and you'll see a gorgeous sight!
   - Ⓙ Avert your eyes often to keep them moist and free of dust particles.

3. **Which word is a synonym for *fastidious*?**
   - Ⓐ jolly
   - Ⓑ agreeable
   - Ⓒ picky
   - Ⓓ calm

4. **Which sentence illustrates the meaning of *lunge*?**
   - Ⓕ The lizard skittered under a bush as I walked past.
   - Ⓖ Dad likes to lie on the couch and watch sports.
   - Ⓗ The fencer raised his foil and attacked his opponent.
   - Ⓙ She didn't see me enter the room and jumped when I spoke.

Writing

Write about a situation in which you might be fastidious. Use **fastidious** in your sentences.

_____

_____

_____

array

noun

1. a large or impressive group or display
2. beautiful or splendid clothing

An **array** of brightly colored flowers lined the parade route. Soon, the queen appeared in royal **array**.

Which definition is being used: "large group" or "splendid clothing"?

- The dancers came on stage in costumes adorned with jewels and feathers.
- The buffet at the wedding had delicacies from all over the world.
- Abigail's dress for the prom was made from silk and lace.
- Our library has the largest selection of books in the city.
- We had a hard time choosing from the extensive menu.

What sort of **array** would you like to wear?

promotion

noun

a move upward in position or grade

My mother's **promotion** at work meant that we could afford music lessons.

Which words mean about the same as **promotion**?

- improvement
- advancement
- demotion
- increase
- decline

Give an example of a **promotion** you can receive at school.

reluctant

adjective

unwilling

The young boy was **reluctant** to jump into the deep end of the pool.

Complete this graphic organizer for **reluctant**.

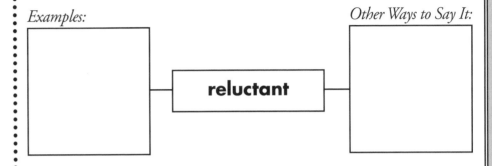

Examples:

reluctant

Other Ways to Say It:

Give an example of something you are **reluctant** to do.

confront

verb

to meet or face boldly

I decided to **confront** my brother about using my bike without permission.

Which word or words mean about the same as **confront**?

- hide
- avoid
- tackle
- deal with
- meet head-on

Tell about a time when you had to **confront** someone about something. What was it about, and what happened?

array • promotion • reluctant • confront

Write on the board the four words studied this week. Read the words with the class and briefly review their meanings. Then conduct the oral activities below.

1 Tell students that you are going to give them a clue about one of the words for the week. They are to find the word that answers the clue.

- When a worker gets one of these, he or she usually receives a pay raise, too. **(a promotion)**

- This word might describe a display of a variety of pastries. **(an array)**

- This word describes someone who isn't at all eager to do something. **(reluctant)**

- You might do this if you suspected someone of stealing from you. **(confront him or her)**

2 Read each sentence and ask students to supply the correct word to complete the sentence.

- The princess's silk and satin ___ was embroidered with glittering jewels. **(array)**

- Should you ___ a bully or just walk away? **(confront)**

- It is raining so hard that I'm ___ to go outside. **(reluctant)**

- Should a student with failing grades receive a ___? **(promotion)**

3 Read each sentence and ask students to tell which word or words are wrong. Then have them provide the correct word from the week's list.

- Mom did such a good job on her project at work that her boss gave her a reprimand. **(reprimand/promotion)**

- I plan to bravely run away from the bully who taunts my sister. **(run away from/confront)**

- My brother is a terrible cook, so I'm always eager to taste his cooking. **(eager/reluctant)**

4 Read each sentence and ask students to decide if it is true or false. If the sentence is false, instruct students to explain why.

- An array is a single object. **(false; it's a group of objects)**

- Most people are reluctant to eat desserts. **(false; most are eager to eat them)**

- It can be scary to confront someone. **(true)**

- Most workers hope for a promotion. **(true)**

Answers for page 35: 1. D, 2. G, 3. A, 4. G

Review Words   array • promotion • reluctant • confront

Fill in the bubble next to the correct answer.

1. **Which word is an antonym for *reluctant*?**
    - Ⓐ bored
    - Ⓑ undecided
    - Ⓒ unwilling
    - Ⓓ eager

2. **Who is most likely to receive a *promotion*?**
    - Ⓕ someone who is celebrating a birthday
    - Ⓖ someone who does a very good job at work
    - Ⓗ someone who needs to improve
    - Ⓙ someone who retired from his or her job last year

3. **Which word is a synonym for *array*?**
    - Ⓐ display
    - Ⓑ pair
    - Ⓒ trio
    - Ⓓ basket

4. **Which phrase could be used instead of *confront* in this sentence?**
    Not being one to <u>confront</u> a bully, Ramon turned and left the room.
    - Ⓕ take a break
    - Ⓖ stand up to someone
    - Ⓗ stand around
    - Ⓙ have fun

Writing

Write about the best way to confront someone without making him or her angry.
Use **confront** in your sentences.

_____

_____

_____

sensitive

adjective

physically or emotionally responsive

Because Felix is so **sensitive** to pollen, we need to be **sensitive** about bringing flowers into the house.

Which people are being **sensitive**?

- Sarah broke out in hives after she ate strawberries.
- Richard is very touchy about wearing glasses.
- Lee shrugged and said, "Oh well, it doesn't matter."
- If the teacher even looks at her questioningly, Laura cries.
- The housekeeper wore gloves when using the strong cleaning agent.

Name an example of a time when it is important to be **sensitive**? When doesn't it really matter?

ambiguous

adjective

having more than one possible meaning

synonym: vague

The judge asked the witness to clarify her **ambiguous** answer.

Which words mean about the same as **ambiguous**?

- uncertain
- confusing
- definite
- unclear
- sure

What questions could you ask if you receive information that is **ambiguous**?

encumber

verb

to weigh down
or burden

The escaping robber was **encumbered** by the heavy sack of loot.

Complete this graphic organizer for **encumber**.

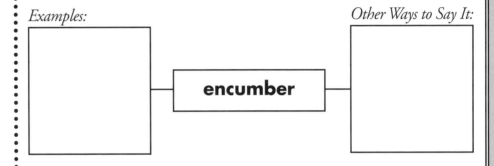

Examples:

Other Ways to Say It:

encumber

Give examples of things that might **encumber** someone from moving freely.

benefactor

noun

someone who gives
generous assistance
or a gift of money

Mr. Lawson was one of the major **benefactors** for the new community swimming pool.

Which words describe a **benefactor**?

- helpful
- kind
- stingy
- thoughtful
- selfish

If you could be a **benefactor**, what kind of help would you like to give and to whom?

sensitive • ambiguous • encumber • benefactor

Write on the board the four words studied this week. Read the words with the class and briefly review their meanings. Then conduct the oral activities below.

1 Tell students that you are going to give them a clue about one of the words for the week. They are to find the word that answers the clue.

- Heavy bags of groceries do this to shoppers. **(encumber them)**

- This is someone who gives money to charity. **(a benefactor)**

- This word describes a sentence with more than one possible meaning. **(ambiguous)**

- This word describes someone who sneezes when smelling perfume. **(sensitive)**

2 Read each sentence and ask students to supply the correct word to complete the sentence.

- When I received a private scholarship, I asked if I could meet my ____. **(benefactor)**

- Heavy backpacks ____ the climbers as they ascend the mountain. **(encumber)**

- Please clarify what you mean by that ____ reply. **(ambiguous)**

- Don't be so ____. I was just kidding you. **(sensitive)**

3 Read each sentence and ask students to tell which word or words are wrong. Then have them provide the correct word from the week's list.

- Her comment was very clear, so I had no idea what she meant. **(very clear/ambiguous)**

- Which of our recipients donated a million dollars to the school fund? **(recipients/benefactors)**

- I hate to lighten your burden with another heavy suitcase. **(lighten your burden/encumber you)**

- She is so hardhearted that she sobs during every sad movie. **(hardhearted/sensitive)**

4 Read each sentence and ask students to decide if it is true or false. If the sentence is false, instruct students to explain why.

- Most dogs have very sensitive ears and noses. **(true)**

- It is easy to answer an ambiguous question. **(false; such a question is unclear)**

- Most people feel grateful to their benefactors. **(true)**

- A pound of feathers and a pound of sand would encumber you equally. **(true)**

Answers for page 39: 1. C, 2. H, 3. A, 4. G

Review Words   sensitive • ambiguous • encumber • benefactor

Fill in the bubble next to the correct answer.

1. **Which word is a synonym for *ambiguous*?**
   - Ⓐ boring
   - Ⓑ clear
   - Ⓒ vague
   - Ⓓ specific

2. **Which set of adjectives best describes a *benefactor*?**
   - Ⓕ selfish, greedy, self-centered, unkind
   - Ⓖ intelligent, well-educated, clever, smart
   - Ⓗ generous, charitable, unselfish, kind
   - Ⓙ poor, unlucky, needy, penniless, broke

3. **Which word is a synonym for *encumber*?**
   - Ⓐ burden
   - Ⓑ assist
   - Ⓒ trick
   - Ⓓ confuse

4. **Which is true of someone who is *sensitive* to smells?**
   - Ⓕ He or she has an extremely poor sense of smell.
   - Ⓖ He or she has a highly developed sense of smell.
   - Ⓗ He or she enjoys all smells—even unpleasant odors.
   - Ⓙ He or she loves fragrant soaps, shampoos, and lotions.

Writing

Write about the things or situations that you are sensitive to. Use **sensitive** in your sentences.

_____

_____

_____

indispensable

adjective

absolutely necessary

Although we can live a long time without food, water is **indispensable**.

Complete this graphic organizer for **indispensable**.

Examples:

Other Ways to Say It:

indispensable

What is something that is **indispensable** to you?

mortify

verb

to cause someone to feel terrible embarrassment

At my graduation party, my brother **mortified** me when he began to sing off-key into the karaoke machine.

How might someone who is **mortified** feel?

- comfortable
- humiliated
- confident
- humbled
- ashamed

Tell about a time when you felt **mortified**. What made you feel **mortified**?

finance

noun

affairs related to money

verb

to provide money for someone or something

My mother has been very successful in **finance**. The profits from her investments helped **finance** our family's restaurant.

Which definition is being used: "affairs related to money" or "to provide money"?

- Students often take on part-time jobs to help finance their college education.
- Being wise about finances enabled Mr. Lee to retire at the age of 50.
- I saved enough money from mowing lawns to finance a new bike.
- Mom adjusted our finances in order to buy a new car.
- Most people need to borrow to finance buying a house.

What is something you would like to **finance**? How do you plan to **finance** it?

bountiful

adjective

more than enough

synonym: plenty

Because everyone brought something to eat, we had a **bountiful** amount of food for the potluck.

Which of these natural elements are **bountiful**?

- crude oil
- pearls
- salt water
- grass
- trees

What is something **bountiful** in your life?

indispensable • mortify • finance • bountiful

Write on the board the four words studied this week. Read the words with the class and briefly review their meanings. Then conduct the oral activities below.

1 Tell students that you are going to give them a clue about one of the words for the week. They are to find the word that answers the clue.

- This word describes a successful harvest. **(bountiful)**

- This word describes something we can't live without, such as air or water. **(indispensable)**

- When you do this to someone, you embarrass that person a great deal. **(mortify him or her)**

- Money managers work in this field. **(finance)**

2 Read each sentence and ask students to supply the correct word to complete the sentence.

- Chloe must work to ____ her trip to Hawaii next summer. **(finance)**

- My parents often ____ me by calling me "sweetie" in public. **(mortify)**

- Drinking water is ____ on a long hike. **(indispensable)**

- We had a ____ apple harvest this year. Every visitor of ours went home with a bag full of apples. **(bountiful)**

3 Read each sentence and ask students to tell which word is wrong. Then have them provide the correct word from the week's list.

- If you want to avoid loneliness, friendships are unnecessary. **(unnecessary/indispensable)**

- Unfortunately, ants were almost as scarce as food at the picnic. **(scarce/bountiful)**

- It delights me when Mom calls me "cutie" in front of my friends. **(delights/mortifies)**

4 Read each sentence and ask students to decide if it is true or false. If the sentence is false, instruct students to explain why.

- Air and water are indispensable to living things. **(true)**

- It mortifies some people to trip and stumble in public. **(true)**

- Food is bountiful at most Thanksgiving dinners. **(true)**

- The field of finance has to do with education. **(false; it has to do with money)**

Answers for page 43: 1. C, 2. J, 3. A, 4. H

Review Words	indispensable • mortify • finance • bountiful

Fill in the bubble next to the correct answer.

1. **Which word is a synonym for *bountiful*?**
   Ⓐ expensive
   Ⓑ delicious
   Ⓒ plentiful
   Ⓓ scarce

2. **If you *mortify* someone, how do you make that person feel?**
   Ⓕ hopeful
   Ⓖ sorrowful
   Ⓗ interested
   Ⓙ embarrassed

3. **Which word is an antonym for *indispensable*?**
   Ⓐ unnecessary
   Ⓑ uncomfortable
   Ⓒ unsatisfied
   Ⓓ undone

4. **When someone *finances* a business, what does he or she provide?**
   Ⓕ leadership
   Ⓖ creativity
   Ⓗ money
   Ⓙ customers

Writing

Write about a special dinner that you would serve if you were hosting friends and family members. Use **bountiful** in your sentences.

_____

_____

_____

endorse

verb

1. to give support or approval to
2. to sign one's name

Famous athletes sometimes **endorse** athletic gear. They have to **endorse** a contract to make a legal agreement with a sporting gear company.

Which definition is being used: "to give support" or "to sign one's name"?

- Do you think the movie star actually follows the diet plan she endorses?
- Both of us must endorse these loan papers from the bank.
- The school's dance team and swim club endorse Michelle for class president.
- I hope you will endorse my petition to put fudge brownies on the lunch menu.
- The principal absolutely does not endorse bullying behavior.

Name some famous people and the products they **endorse**.

idle

adjective

not busy; doing nothing

synonym: lazy

I like to spend my **idle** hours on a rainy day watching old movies.

Would you be **idle** if you were:

- swinging in a hammock?
- water-skiing?
- sunbathing?
- canoeing?
- napping?

What do you like to do during your **idle** time?

descend

verb

to move from a higher place to a lower place

The squirrel quickly **descended** from the treetop to the ground.

Complete this graphic organizer for **descend**.

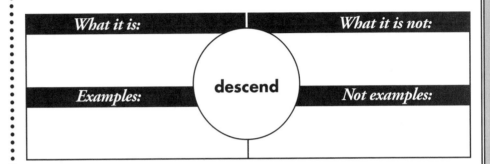

What it is:		What it is not:
Examples:	descend	Not examples:

From what high place have you **descended**?

absorb

verb

1. to involve or engage completely
2. to take in or soak up

Marta is **absorbed** by an interest in horses. She **absorbs** all the books she can find on the subject.

The following words are synonyms for **absorb**. Which meaning is being used: "to engage completely" or "to take in or soak up"?

- fascinate
- comprehend
- digest
- involve
- mesmerize

What is the best way for you to **absorb** new information? Do you like to read, listen, or view as a way to **absorb** information?

Review

endorse • idle • descend • absorb

Write on the board the four words studied this week. Read the words with the class and briefly review their meanings. Then conduct the oral activities below.

1 Tell students that you are going to give them a clue about one of the words for the week. They are to find the word that answers the clue.

- You do this when you ride a "down" escalator. (**descend**)

- When you memorize information, you do this. (**absorb it**)

- People do this when they sign checks. (**endorse them**)

- This word describes someone who isn't doing anything. (**idle**)

2 Read each sentence and ask students to supply the correct word to complete the sentence.

- Except when she's asleep, Mom is rarely ____. (**idle**)

- When a candidate loses a political party's nomination, he or she may publicly ____ a former opponent. (**endorse**)

- My three-year-old cousin is quick to ____ any information about dinosaurs. (**absorb**)

- Let's use the stairs to ____ from the third to the first floor. (**descend**)

3 Read each sentence and ask students to tell which word is wrong. Then have them provide the correct word from the week's list.

- Let's use the elevator to ascend from the second floor to the basement. (**ascend/descend**)

- Dad spends his work hours daydreaming or surfing the Web on his computer. (**work/idle**)

- I can't read enough fantasy books! The fantasy genre bores me. (**bores/absorbs**)

- The Nutzy Peanut Butter company paid a movie star to criticize its product. (**criticize/endorse**)

4 Read each sentence and ask students to decide if it is true or false. If the sentence is false, instruct students to explain why.

- You are likely to be absorbed by your hobby. (**true**)

- Helium balloons descend after the helium leaks out. (**true**)

- Political candidates often endorse their opponents. (**false; people running for office do not support those running against them**)

- Many people are idle on weekends. (**true**)

Answers for page 47: 1. D, 2. F, 3. A, 4. G

| **Review Words** | endorse • idle • descend • absorb |

Fill in the bubble next to the correct answer.

1. **Which word is an antonym for *descend*?**
   - Ⓐ dawdle
   - Ⓑ hurry
   - Ⓒ sink
   - Ⓓ rise

2. **Which word is a synonym for *endorse*?**
   - Ⓕ approve
   - Ⓖ criticize
   - Ⓗ question
   - Ⓙ analyze

3. **In which sentence could *idle* be used to fill in the blank?**
   - Ⓐ After doing yardwork all day, it felt good to be ____ that evening.
   - Ⓑ Shouldn't you get busy and quit doing ____?
   - Ⓒ People who read lots of books have ____ minds.
   - Ⓓ I think I'll be ____ and bake pies for dessert.

4. **Which word could be used instead of *absorb* in this sentence?**

   The speech was so full of scientific terminology that I could <u>absorb</u> little of it.
   - Ⓕ sponge
   - Ⓖ comprehend
   - Ⓗ mesmerize
   - Ⓙ blot

Writing

Write about a product that you would endorse on TV or the radio if you were famous. Use **endorse** in your sentences.

_____

_____

erroneous

adjective

containing an error

antonym: correct

The garage sale address given in the newspaper was **erroneous**, so we never found the right location.

Which of the following statements are **erroneous**?

- The United States is one of the oldest nations on Earth.
- New Mexico is one of the states in the United States.
- Texas is the smallest state in the United States.
- The United States is made up of sixty states.
- The United States is in South America.

What can you do to avoid writing **erroneous** information?

mesmerize

verb

to fascinate

synonym:
to entrance

The meteor shower **mesmerized** everyone who saw it.

Which of the following situations would be likely to **mesmerize** you?

- waiting for your appointment at the dentist's office
- sitting quietly while your parents visited with old friends
- watching a pride of lions while on an African safari
- seeing your favorite singer shopping at the grocery store
- swimming with a pod of dolphins

Tell about a time when you were **mesmerized**.

familiar

adjective

1. well-known; easily recognized
2. knowing something or someone well

I am very **familiar** with this book because I read it last year. Its theme, the challenges of growing up, is a **familiar** one.

Which of the following are **familiar** to you?

- chemistry
- the alphabet
- trigonometry
- your best friend
- your classroom

Give examples of some **familiar** flowers.

jubilant

adjective

feeling or showing great joy

synonym: ecstatic

The streets were filled with **jubilant** spectators as the Olympic victors paraded past.

Complete this graphic organizer for **jubilant**.

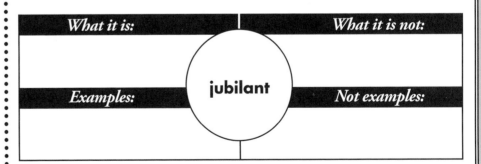

What it is:		*What it is not:*
	jubilant	
Examples:		*Not examples:*

Tell about something that made you feel **jubilant**.

Review

erroneous • mesmerize • familiar • jubilant

Write on the board the four words studied this week. Read the words with the class and briefly review their meanings. Then conduct the oral activities below.

1 Tell students that you are going to give them a clue about one of the words for the week. They are to find the word that answers the clue.

- Many people feel this way at weddings. **(jubilant)**

- This word describes the answer to this problem: 34 + 22 = 58. **(erroneous)**

- Amazing sights do this to some people. **(mesmerize them)**

- This word describes people who you know well. **(familiar)**

2 Read each sentence and ask students to supply the correct word to complete the sentence.

- When I returned to my old hometown, it felt good to walk down ___ streets. **(familiar)**

- Taylor felt ___ after she won the competition. **(jubilant)**

- That is ___ information. I'm twelve years old, not eleven. **(erroneous)**

- Good dancers can ___ an audience with their beautiful movements. **(mesmerize)**

3 Read each sentence and ask students to tell which word is wrong. Then have them provide the correct word from the week's list.

- It's correct to say that *Mississippi* has nine letters. **(correct/erroneous)**

- When they play interesting roles, good actors bore their audiences. **(bore/mesmerize)**

- Most people at the graduation ceremony felt awful. **(awful/jubilant)**

- Everyone knows his strange face from the local TV news. **(strange/familiar)**

4 Read each sentence and ask students to decide if it is true or false. If the sentence is false, instruct students to explain why.

- A familiar saying is one that most people have heard. **(true)**

- Parents usually feel jubilant when their babies are born. **(true)**

- TV shows can mesmerize viewers. **(true)**

- It's erroneous to say that *navy* is a color. **(false; it's a dark shade of blue)**

Answers for page 51: 1. C, 2. G, 3. B, 4. H

Name _____

Review Words   erroneous • mesmerize • familiar • jubilant

Fill in the bubble next to the correct answer.

1. **Which word is an antonym for *jubilant*?**
   - Ⓐ clever
   - Ⓑ exhausted
   - Ⓒ mournful
   - Ⓓ joyful

2. **Which is an *erroneous* statement?**
   - Ⓕ When you mix yellow and blue, you get green.
   - Ⓖ There are 364 days in an Earth year.
   - Ⓗ A book normally has a front and a back cover.
   - Ⓙ A pencil is a writing implement.

3. **Which word could be used in place of *familiar* in this sentence?**

   I am not <u>familiar</u> with the song you just played.
   - Ⓐ famous
   - Ⓑ acquainted
   - Ⓒ common
   - Ⓓ widespread

4. **Which words are synonyms for *mesmerize*?**
   - Ⓕ transform, change, modify
   - Ⓖ alarm, terrify, horrify
   - Ⓗ entrance, fascinate, hypnotize
   - Ⓙ embrace, cuddle, comfort

Writing

Write about an event you attended at which most people were jubilant. Use **jubilant** in your sentences.

_____

_____

_____

repose

noun

freedom from activity or responsibility

After a long week at school, I find **repose** in lounging on the couch, watching cartoons.

Which words mean about the same as **repose**?

- calmness
- relaxation
- stillness
- frenzy
- chaos

Describe the perfect environment in which to find **repose**.

antique

noun

something made a long time ago

Our dining room table, which we inherited from my great-grandmother, is an **antique**.

Complete this graphic organizer for **antique**.

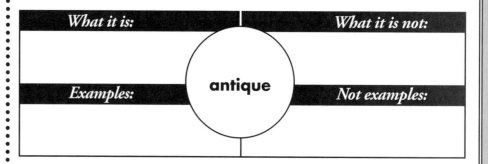

Tell about an **antique** that your family owns or would like to own.

conform

verb

to act or think in a way that follows the rules

I'd rather sit on the floor, but in school I must **conform** and sit at a desk.

Do you **conform** when you act:

- rebellious?
- obediently?
- in a traditional way?
- just like everyone else?
- differently from others?

What is a rule that everyone **conforms** to at school?

fatigue

noun

the condition of being very tired

synonym: exhaustion

I felt extreme **fatigue** after the twenty-mile bike ride.

Which of the following could cause **fatigue**?

- flying in an airplane for 14 hours
- getting a good night's sleep
- staying up to watch the late, late movie
- reading a good book in a comfortable chair
- hiking up a steep mountain trail

What types of activities cause you to feel **fatigue**?

Review

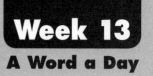

repose • antique • conform • fatigue

Write on the board the four words studied this week. Read the words with the class and briefly review their meanings. Then conduct the oral activities below.

1 Tell students that you are going to give them a clue about one of the words for the week. They are to find the word that answers the clue.

- A dining table built in 1910 is one. **(an antique)**

- You do this when you follow school rules. **(conform)**

- This is what you feel when you are exhausted. **(fatigue)**

- This is what you need when you are exhausted. **(repose)**

2 Read each sentence and ask students to supply the correct word to complete the sentence.

- A rebel won't ____ to other people's rules. **(conform)**

- After the race was over, Alex felt overwhelmed with ____. **(fatigue)**

- A week's vacation will provide Mom with much needed ____. **(repose)**

- This finely carved old chair is an ____ that my family has owned for over 80 years. **(antique)**

3 Read each sentence and ask students to tell which word or words are wrong. Then have them provide the correct word from the week's list.

- Sewn in the 1920s, this dress is the latest style. **(the latest style/an antique)**

- Our teacher wants everyone to rebel against school rules. **(rebel against/conform to)**

- Napping on the couch provides Dad with the exercise he desires. **(exercise/repose)**

- I had no sleep last night, so my eyes are blurred from alertness. **(alertness/fatigue)**

4 Read each sentence and ask students to decide if it is true or false. If the sentence is false, instruct students to explain why.

- Fatigue can prevent people from thinking clearly. **(true)**

- A five-year-old car is an antique. **(false; an antique is generally older than 50 years)**

- Vacations are one way people take repose. **(true)**

- The American Revolution happened because colonists wanted to conform to British laws. **(false; they rebelled against British laws)**

Answers for page 55: 1. B, 2. J, 3. B, 4. H

Review Words repose • antique • conform • fatigue

Fill in the bubble next to the correct answer.

1. **Which word is a synonym for *fatigue*?**
   Ⓐ curiosity
   Ⓑ exhaustion
   Ⓒ mourning
   Ⓓ energy

2. **Which word is an antonym for *conform*?**
   Ⓕ enforce
   Ⓖ obey
   Ⓗ follow
   Ⓙ rebel

3. **Which of the following is an example of being in *repose*?**
   Ⓐ Joey practicing spins on his skateboard
   Ⓑ Gramps reading the newspaper in his hammock
   Ⓒ the family dog digging a hole in the flower bed
   Ⓓ Shannon shooting hoops in the driveway

4. **Which is an *antique*?**
   Ⓕ a car that runs on electricity
   Ⓖ a car that is out of gasoline
   Ⓗ a car that was built in 1935
   Ⓙ a car that was built last year

Writing

Write about a rule you think everyone should conform to. Use **conform** in your sentences.

_____

_____

_____

infinite

adjective

without limits;
without end

The universe contains an **infinite** number
of stars.

Which words have about the same meaning as **infinite**?

- countless
- unlimited
- restricted
- endless
- finite

Give an example of something that is **infinite**.

pucker

verb

to gather or contract
into folds or wrinkles

Your lips might **pucker** when you taste
a lemon.

Which of these illustrate the idea of **pucker**?

- the skin on your fingers after washing a lot of dishes
- lips getting ready to give Grandma a kiss
- a smoothly folded towel
- the surface of a school desk
- the elastic waistband of workout pants

Make an expression by **puckering** your facial features.

adaptation

noun

something that has been changed to fit different conditions

The movie version of *The Lion, the Witch and the Wardrobe* was an excellent **adaptation** of the book.

Which of these describe an **adaptation**?

- a chick raised by a family of ducks
- a book that is presented as a play
- a poem that is turned into a song
- a song performed by a group
- a ghost story read aloud

Give another example of a movie that is an **adaptation** of a book.

urban

adjective

something that is from the city or related to a city

High-rise buildings and taxis are common in **urban** areas.

Complete this graphic organizer for **urban**.

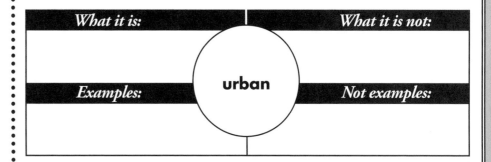

What it is:		*What it is not:*
	urban	
Examples:		*Not examples:*

Describe an **urban** area that you have visited. Would you prefer living in an **urban** setting or some other type of setting?

infinite • pucker • adaptation • urban

Write on the board the four words studied this week. Read the words with the class and briefly review their meanings. Then conduct the oral activities below.

1 Tell students that you are going to give them a clue about one of the words for the week. They are to find the word that answers the clue.

- Your lips do this when you taste something sour. **(pucker)**

- This word describes an unlimited amount. **(infinite)**

- This word describes areas that have subways and skyscrapers. **(urban)**

- A TV show based on a movie is one. **(an adaptation)**

2 Read each sentence and ask students to supply the correct word to complete the sentence.

- Did you think the movie *A Wrinkle in Time* was a good ____ of the book? **(adaptation)**

- If you aren't careful when you hang wallpaper, it will ____. **(pucker)**

- Although the number of ants in the world is huge, it is not ____. **(infinite)**

- Ms. Huntley prefers the excitement of ____ life to a calmer small-town existence. **(urban)**

3 Read each sentence and ask students to tell which word or words are wrong. Then have them provide the correct word from the week's list.

- Traffic is one negative aspect of country life. **(country/urban)**

- Aunt Rose smoothed out her lips and kissed me on the cheek. **(smoothed out/puckered)**

- Molly never loses her temper. She has a limited amount of patience. **(a limited/an infinite)**

4 Read each sentence and ask students to decide if it is true or false. If the sentence is false, instruct students to explain why.

- A movie based on a play is an adaptation. **(true)**

- Most urban areas are sparsely populated. **(false; most cities are crowded with people)**

- *Pucker* and *relax* are antonyms. **(true)**

- *Infinite* and *endless* are synonyms. **(true)**

Answers for page 59: 1. A, 2. G, 3. D, 4. H

Name _____

Fill in the bubble next to the correct answer.

1. Which word is an antonym for *urban*?

(A) rural

(B) modern

(C) old-fashioned

(D) citified

2. Which word is an antonym for *infinite*?

(F) limitless

(G) limited

(H) certain

(J) iffy

3. Which of these is an *adaptation*?

(A) a movie about a talking horse

(B) a poem about the poet's family

(C) a folk song about war and peace

(D) a TV show based on a folk tale

4. In which sentence could *pucker* be used to fill in the blank?

(F) Use a _____ to rearrange the logs in the fire.

(G) Running ten miles is sure to _____ us out.

(H) Smooth the front of your shirt so it doesn't _____.

(J) Help me _____ the clothes that I just took out of the dryer.

Writing

Write about something you'd like to have an infinite amount of. Use **infinite** in your sentences.

_____

_____

_____

converge

verb

to come together

synonym: to merge

Main Street and Elm Street **converge** at the center of town.

Complete this graphic organizer for **converge**.

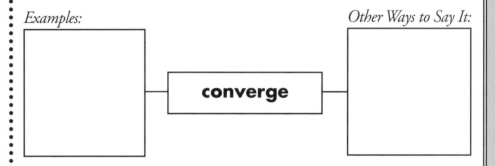

Examples: *Other Ways to Say It:*

converge

What are some things besides streets that **converge**?

sarcastic

adjective

using cutting or bitter words for the purpose of making fun of someone or something

I was already embarrassed about my bad haircut, and my classmates' **sarcastic** remarks didn't make me feel any better.

Which words mean about the same as **sarcastic**?

- biting
- scornful
- soothing
- mocking
- encouraging

How would you respond to someone who made a **sarcastic** comment to you? How could you let him or her know that you don't like hearing **sarcastic** words?

esteem

noun

a very positive opinion

synonym: respect

Anita was held in high **esteem** because of all her volunteer work in the community.

Which word or words have about the same meaning as **esteem**?

- admiration
- scorn
- approval
- honor
- high regard

What does it mean to have **self-esteem**? How does **self-esteem** feel?

cavort

verb

to run and jump around playfully

The children love to **cavort** in the sprinklers on hot afternoons.

Which word or words mean about the same as **cavort**?

- prance about
- sit down
- frolic
- play
- nap

When and where do you like to **cavort**?

converge • sarcastic • esteem • cavort

Write on the board the four words studied this week. Read the words with the class and briefly review their meanings. Then conduct the oral activities below.

1 Tell students that you are going to give them a clue about one of the words for the week. They are to find the word that answers the clue.

- Lambs, colts, and baby goats do this. **(cavort)**

- This is what you feel for someone whom you greatly respect. **(esteem)**

- This word describes a comment that is meant to be hurtful. **(sarcastic)**

- Two rivers do this when they come together. **(converge)**

2 Read each sentence and ask students to supply the correct word to complete the sentence.

- Leo's ____ comments hurt my feelings. **(sarcastic)**

- I hold good writers such as J. K. Rowling in high ____. **(esteem)**

- I love to watch my kittens ____ about the room. **(cavort)**

- Parallel lines run side by side and do not ____. **(converge)**

3 Read each sentence and ask students to tell which word is wrong. Then have them provide the correct word from the week's list.

- When two streams separate, they form a wider stream. **(separate/converge)**

- Don't be so encouraging, or you may hurt people's feelings. **(encouraging/sarcastic)**

- I hold Matt in great contempt. He is the smartest person I know. **(contempt/esteem)**

4 Read each sentence and ask students to decide if it is true or false. If the sentence is false, instruct students to explain why.

- Sick, tired, or grumpy children don't usually cavort with friends. **(true)**

- If you disrespect someone, you hold him or her in high esteem. **(false; the opposite is true)**

- *Converge* and *divide* are synonyms. **(false; they are antonyms)**

- *Sarcastic* and *mocking* are synonyms. **(true)**

Answers for page 63: 1. C, 2. J, 3. B, 4. H

Review Words   converge • sarcastic • esteem • cavort

Fill in the bubble next to the correct answer.

1. Which word is an antonym for *esteem*?

Ⓐ affection

Ⓑ trust

Ⓒ contempt

Ⓓ respect

2. Which word is an antonym for *converge*?

Ⓕ begin

Ⓖ multiply

Ⓗ conclude

Ⓙ separate

3. If someone broke a glass, which would be a *sarcastic* response?

Ⓐ "That was my favorite glass!"

Ⓑ "Hey, good job, Graceful."

Ⓒ "Are you OK? Did you cut yourself?"

Ⓓ "Don't worry—we have a lot more."

4. When might someone *cavort* around a room?

Ⓕ when he or she is exhausted

Ⓖ when he or she is furious

Ⓗ when he or she feels joyful

Ⓙ when he or she feels mournful

Writing

Write to explain why you think people make sarcastic comments. Use **sarcastic** in your sentences.

_____

_____

_____

vehement

adjective

expressing strong feelings

synonym: intense

She was **vehement** about finishing the project by herself.

Which of the following are **vehement** statements?

- "I will never ever talk to you again."
- "I am absolutely convinced of it."
- "Stop it immediately!"
- "It doesn't matter to me."
- "Whatever."

Give an example of something you are **vehement** about.

restoration

noun

the act of bringing something back to its original condition

The **restoration** of the old house took more than a year.

Which of these phrases have about the same meaning as **restoration**?

- to let fall into ruin
- to fix up like new
- to run down
- to rebuild
- to repair

Give examples of some places or things that have gone through **restoration**.

queue

noun

a line formed
for waiting

The **queue** to buy tickets wrapped all around the theater and extended into the parking lot.

In which of the following situations might you find a **queue**?

- waiting to board a jumbo jet
- at a concession stand at a ballpark
- in your living room
- at a busy bus stop
- outside a department store about to open for a half-price sale

What is the longest **queue** you've ever waited in?

amuse

verb

1. to entertain
2. to cause to smile or laugh

The boys read comic books to **amuse** themselves during the long cross-country flight. The antics of the comic-book characters **amused** them.

Complete this graphic organizer for **amuse**.

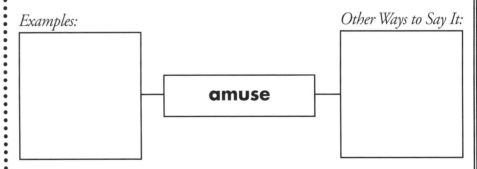

Examples:

Other Ways to Say It:

amuse

Give examples of things you do to **amuse** yourself on rainy weekends.

vehement • restoration • queue • amuse

Write on the board the four words studied this week. Read the words with the class and briefly review their meanings. Then conduct the oral activities below.

1 Tell students that you are going to give them a clue about one of the words for the week. They are to find the word that answers the clue.

- You might wait in one to buy tickets. (**a queue**)

- Entertainers try to do this to audiences. (**amuse them**)

- This word describes a statement such as "I absolutely despise broccoli!" (**vehement**)

- Old buildings that are in disrepair need this. (**restoration**)

2 Read each sentence and ask students to supply the correct word to complete the sentence.

- Many carpenters, plumbers, and electricians worked on the building's _____. (**restoration**)

- Few activities _____ me more than reading. (**amuse**)

- To buy concert tickets, we waited in a _____ for over an hour. (**queue**)

- The attorney was _____ in her defense of her client. (**vehement**)

3 Read each sentence and ask students to tell which word is wrong. Then have them provide the correct word from the week's list.

- His casual statement showed his deep feelings on the topic. (**casual/vehement**)

- Artists worked for months on the old mural's destruction. (**destruction/restoration**)

- The magician hoped to bore his audience with several new tricks. (**bore/amuse**)

4 Read each sentence and ask students to decide if it is true or false. If the sentence is false, instruct students to explain why.

- *Queue* and *line* are synonyms. (**true**)

- A vehement statement shows that the speaker doesn't care. (**false; if you are vehement, you care passionately about the subject**)

- *Restoration* and *demolition* are antonyms. (**true**)

- *Amuse* and *entertain* are synonyms. (**true**)

Answers for page 67: 1. C, 2. G, 3. B, 4. F

Name _____

Fill in the bubble next to the correct answer.

1. Which word is an antonym for *amuse*?

Ⓐ despise

Ⓑ teach

Ⓒ bore

Ⓓ entertain

2. Which word is an antonym for *restoration*?

Ⓕ commencement

Ⓖ destruction

Ⓗ development

Ⓙ construction

3. Who is most likely to make a *vehement* statement?

Ⓐ someone who doesn't care about the topic

Ⓑ someone who cares deeply about the topic

Ⓒ someone who is unfamiliar with the topic

Ⓓ someone who feels bored by the topic

4. Who is most likely to wait in a *queue*?

Ⓕ someone who is waiting to buy movie tickets

Ⓖ someone who is waiting for a friend to phone

Ⓗ someone who is waiting for summer to arrive

Ⓙ someone who is waiting for a friend to come over

Writing

Write about a reason you would be willing to wait in a very long queue. Tell what you'd do as you waited. Use **queue** in your sentences.

_____

_____

_____

dedicate

verb

to set apart for a special purpose or use

synonym: devote

We will **dedicate** the new building for use as a computer lab.

Complete this graphic organizer for **dedicate**.

Examples: *Other Ways to Say It:*

dedicate

If you had some land that you could **dedicate** for a special use, what would that use be?

glare

verb

to stare in an angry way

noun

a strong, bright light

The driver **glared** at us when my mom pulled out in front of him. She didn't see him because of the **glare** on the windshield.

Which definition is being used: "to stare angrily" or "a strong, bright light"?

- The glare off the water made me squint.
- Adrianne's glare told me not to take a piece of her chocolate chip cookie.
- The principal glared at the rowdy students who were throwing paper airplanes during the assembly.
- I would have caught that fly ball if it weren't for the glare in my eyes!
- Mom can silence my sister and me with nothing more than a glare.

Show how you look when you **glare** at someone.

utter

verb

to make an audible sound with your voice

We tried not to **utter** a sound as we watched the deer and her fawn walk through our backyard.

Which of these are sounds you could **utter**?

- a sigh
- a thud
- a cough
- a splash
- a scream

What was one of the first words you **uttered** when you learned to speak?

compose

verb

1. to become calm
2. to create by putting together words or musical notes

The pianist took a moment to **compose** himself before he stepped onstage to perform the music he had **composed**.

Which definition is being used: "to become calm" or "to create by putting together words or musical notes"?

- I had to compose myself before meeting my favorite baseball player.
- Many famous singers do not compose their own songs.
- Ramona could not compose herself when she heard that she won first prize.
- The guitarist composed all the pieces on his latest CD.
- Just compose yourself! Losing one game isn't the end of the world.

What do you do to **compose** yourself when you are getting too upset or excited?

dedicate • glare • utter • compose

Write on the board the four words studied this week. Read the words with the class and briefly review their meanings. Then conduct the oral activities below.

1 Tell students that you are going to give them a clue about one of the words for the week. They are to find the word that answers the clue.

- Hats and sunglasses protect your eyes from this. **(glare)**

- Poets do this. **(compose poetry)**

- You do this with words when you speak. **(utter them)**

- You do this when you devote some time to a specific purpose. **(dedicate time to it)**

2 Read each sentence and ask students to supply the correct word to complete the sentence.

- I wish you wouldn't ____ at me like that. What did I do to anger you? **(glare)**

- This summer, I'm going to ____ some time to reorganizing my bedroom. **(dedicate)**

- I was nervous before giving the speech, so I took some time to ____ myself. **(compose)**

- I was so surprised that I couldn't ____ a word. **(utter)**

3 Read each sentence and ask students to tell which word or words are wrong. Then have them provide the correct word from the week's list.

- Soft music can help people stir up their feelings. **(stir up/compose)**

- Don't hold back a sound! We don't want to wake the baby! **(hold back/utter)**

- I always smile at drivers who don't stop for me when I am in a crosswalk. **(smile/glare)**

4 Read each sentence and ask students to decide if it is true or false. If the sentence is false, instruct students to explain why.

- When you volunteer, you dedicate some time to help others. **(true)**

- It is easy for drivers to see when there is a glare on their windshields. **(false; it is hard for them to see)**

- Some musicians compose music. **(true)**

- Strong feelings such as joy, terror, or amazement can make it hard to utter sounds. **(true)**

Answers for page 71: 1. A, 2. F, 3. C, 4. H

Name _____

Fill in the bubble next to the correct answer.

1. Which word expresses the opposite idea of *glare*?

Ⓐ grin

Ⓑ frown

Ⓒ shout

Ⓓ whisper

2. Which word is a synonym for *utter*?

Ⓕ say

Ⓖ swallow

Ⓗ understand

Ⓙ ignore

3. Who or what is most likely to *compose* music?

Ⓐ a listener

Ⓑ a violin

Ⓒ a musician

Ⓓ a concert hall

4. In which sentence could *dedicated* be used to fill in the blank?

Ⓕ I ____ you to be the playground ball monitor.

Ⓖ The class ____ some clothing to the homeless shelter.

Ⓗ The land along the river will be ____ for a park.

Ⓙ We ____ a strange smell coming from the refrigerator.

Writing

Write about a goal to which you plan to dedicate time. Use **dedicate** in your sentences.

_____

_____

_____

volunteer

noun

a person who chooses to work without being paid

The Red Cross counts on many **volunteers** to help out during natural disasters.

Which of these people **volunteer**?

- The scouts cleared hiking trails in the park last weekend.
- Hector earned $25.00 caring for his neighbor's dog.
- Dad got a $1.50 per hour raise.
- The aquarium appreciates the help of unpaid docents.
- On Saturdays, I give a few hours to groom dogs at the animal shelter.

What sort of work would you be willing to do as a **volunteer**?

pessimistic

adjective

expecting things to turn out badly

antonym: optimistic

Andrea is so **pessimistic**! She is sure that it will rain on the day of the class picnic.

Which words mean about the same as **pessimistic**?

- excited
- gloomy
- cheerful
- negative
- despairing

Do you think you are a **pessimistic** person? Explain why or why not.

detest

verb

to dislike very much

I know that spinach contains lots of iron and is a healthy food, but I still **detest** it.

Complete this graphic organizer for **detest**.

Examples: *Other Ways to Say It:*

detest

What is something you **detest**? Why do you dislike it so much?

tolerant

adjective

willing to respect people who think or act differently than you

To have a harmonious classroom, we all need to recognize and be **tolerant** of our differences.

Which words best describe someone who is **tolerant**?

- open-minded
- hateful
- accepting
- gossiping
- understanding

How would you encourage others to be **tolerant**?

volunteer • pessimistic • detest • tolerant

Write on the board the four words studied this week. Read the words with the class and briefly review their meanings. Then conduct the oral activities below.

1 Tell students that you are going to give them a clue about one of the words for the week. They are to find the word that answers the clue.

- This word describes someone who has a habit of expecting bad outcomes. **(pessimistic)**

- If you get along with people of many different personalities and beliefs, this word describes you. **(tolerant)**

- You feel this way about foods that you hate. **(you detest them)**

- This is someone who does unpaid work to help others. **(a volunteer)**

2 Read each sentence and ask students to supply the correct word to complete the sentence.

- I work as a _____ in a senior citizens' center. **(volunteer)**

- It's just as easy to be optimistic as it is to be _____. **(pessimistic)**

- Some people _____ vegetables as kids, but grow to love them as adults. **(detest)**

- You will avoid arguments if you are _____ of other people's views. **(tolerant)**

3 Read each sentence and ask students to tell which word is wrong. Then have them provide the correct word from the week's list.

- I adore slimy foods—they make me sick. **(adore/detest)**

- Don't be so optimistic! You have a better chance of winning than you think. **(optimistic/pessimistic)**

- Prejudiced people respect other cultures' beliefs and customs. **(Prejudiced/Tolerant)**

4 Read each sentence and ask students to decide if it is true or false. If the sentence is false, instruct students to explain why.

- Most volunteers receive pay. **(false; most are unpaid)**

- A pessimistic person looks on the bright side. **(false; he or she expects a bad outcome)**

- Racists are tolerant people. **(false; they are intolerant)**

- *Detest* and *love* are antonyms. **(true)**

Answers for page 75: 1. D, 2. F, 3. D, 4. G

Review Words	volunteer • pessimistic • detest • tolerant

Fill in the bubble next to the correct answer.

1. **Which word is an antonym for *detest*?**
   - Ⓐ great
   - Ⓑ pity
   - Ⓒ despise
   - Ⓓ adore

2. **Which word is a synonym for *tolerant*?**
   - Ⓕ accepting
   - Ⓖ enthusiastic
   - Ⓗ terrified
   - Ⓙ skeptical

3. **Which weather prediction is a *pessimistic* person most likely to make?**
   - Ⓐ "Don't worry—it won't rain on the day of our picnic."
   - Ⓑ "I hope it won't rain, but it's hard to predict, isn't it?"
   - Ⓒ "It looks like rain, but maybe it will clear up in time."
   - Ⓓ "I just know it will rain and completely ruin our picnic."

4. **Which adjectives best describe a *volunteer*?**
   - Ⓕ paid, greedy, selfish, grumpy, mean
   - Ⓖ unpaid, kind, generous, unselfish
   - Ⓗ professional, efficient, wealthy, smart
   - Ⓙ incompetent, sloppy, lazy, messy, untidy

Writing

Write about the most pessimistic person you know. Explain how he or she displays this trait. Use **pessimistic** in your sentences.

_____

_____

_____

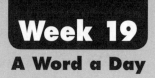

ultimate

adjective

final

synonym: last

When the bus reached its **ultimate** destination, only two passengers remained.

Complete this graphic organizer for **ultimate**.

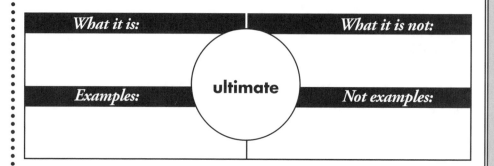

What is your **ultimate** educational goal?

ventilation

noun

the circulation of air

The cabin was hot and stuffy because there was no **ventilation**.

Which of these help provide **ventilation**?

- a fan
- a sunroof
- new curtains
- open windows
- air conditioning

How do you get **ventilation** in your house?

anonymous

adjective

from someone whose name is not known

The ancient Greek poem is by an **anonymous** author.

Which of these could be **anonymous**?

- a phone call
- a newspaper
- an admirer
- graffiti
- an autograph

Why do you think newspapers don't print articles written by **anonymous** writers?

know-how

noun

the knowledge of how to do something

A carpenter has real **know-how** when it comes to building things.

Which words mean about the same as **know-how**?

- ignorance
- mastery
- difficulty
- ability
- skill

In what areas do you have real **know-how**?

ultimate • ventilation • anonymous • know-how

Write on the board the four words studied this week. Read the words with the class and briefly review their meanings. Then conduct the oral activities below.

1 Tell students that you are going to give them a clue about one of the words for the week. They are to find the word that answers the clue.

- You need this to do a job quickly and well. (**know-how**)

- This word describes an unknown writer. (**anonymous**)

- This word describes the last step in a series. (**ultimate**)

- Open windows help to provide this. (**ventilation**)

2 Read each sentence and ask students to supply the correct word to complete the sentence.

- An ____ donor sent us the money, so we weren't able to thank him or her. (**anonymous**)

- Mom's plumbing ____ comes in handy when our pipes are clogged. (**know-how**)

- Dad installed fans to provide better ____. (**ventilation**)

- Dying in combat is the ____ sacrifice that a soldier can make. (**ultimate**)

3 Read each sentence and ask students to tell which word is wrong. Then have them provide the correct word from the week's list.

- Eight-year-old Sam is a Cub Scout, whose first goal is to be an Eagle Scout. (**first/ultimate**)

- The work is by a well-known painter. Unfortunately, we will never know the artist's name. (**a well-known/an anonymous**)

- When it comes to cooking, Dad's ignorance is amazing—he's an experienced chef. (**ignorance/know-how**)

4 Read each sentence and ask students to decide if it is true or false. If the sentence is false, instruct students to explain why.

- A tightly sealed glass jar has no ventilation inside. (**true**)

- The ultimate alphabet letter is *L*. (**false;** *Z* **is the last letter**)

- The *Harry Potter* books are by an anonymous author. (**false; J.K. Rowling wrote them**)

- *Know-how* and *skill* are synonyms. (**true**)

Answers for page 79: 1. C, 2. H, 3. A, 4. J

Review Words ultimate • ventilation • anonymous • know-how

Fill in the bubble next to the correct answer.

1. **Which word is a synonym for *anonymous*?**
   - (A) deceased
   - (B) talented
   - (C) unnamed
   - (D) famous

2. **What will happen in a room with no *ventilation*?**
   - (F) People won't be able to see well.
   - (G) It will be too noisy to hear properly.
   - (H) There won't be enough fresh air.
   - (J) People won't be able to watch TV.

3. **Which word is an antonym for *know-how*?**
   - (A) ignorance
   - (B) knowledge
   - (C) trust
   - (D) suspicion

4. **Which is the *ultimate* chapter in a book with fifty chapters?**
   - (F) Chapter 1
   - (G) Chapter 2
   - (H) Chapter 25
   - (J) Chapter 50

Writing

Write about someone in your family who has know-how in a certain area.
Use **know-how** in your sentences.

_____

_____

_____

stratosphere

noun

the layer of atmosphere that extends from about 11 miles to 30 miles above Earth

The **stratosphere** contains the ozone layer, which absorbs solar radiation, helping the temperatures in the **stratosphere** to remain fairly constant.

Which of these might you expect to find in the **stratosphere**?

- birds
- aliens
- very few clouds
- thin air
- weather balloons

Do you think it will ever be common to travel through Earth's **stratosphere**? What might that be like?

endow

verb

1. to provide with an ability, talent, or other positive qualities at birth

2. to give money or property to

The scientist was **endowed** with an astounding ability to invent new technologies. With his fortune, he has **endowed** science programs in many schools.

Which definition is being used: "to provide with an ability or quality" or "to give money or property to"?

- The twins were both endowed with musical talent.
- Our class president is endowed with a lot of charm.
- A benefactor endowed the museum with land on which to expand the building.
- People often leave money in their wills to endow the schools they attended.
- The U.S. Constitution states that we are endowed with certain inalienable rights.

What special abilities are you **endowed** with?

charisma

noun

an unusual ability to influence people and inspire devotion

Kali's **charisma** made her a popular choice for class president.

Which of these people display **charisma**?

- He is so opinionated, no one wants to work with him.
- She is a leader who inspires people to follow her.
- Her pessimistic attitude is hard to take.
- The candidate's speech had the audience on its feet cheering.
- The entire country mourned the death of the beloved singer.

Describe someone you know or a public figure who has **charisma**.

ancient

adjective

from times long past

The **ancient** pyramids of Egypt still stand today.

Complete this graphic organizer for **ancient**.

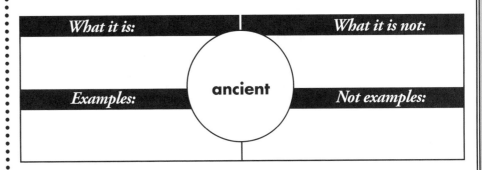

What it is:		*What it is not:*
	ancient	
Examples:		*Not examples:*

What is something **ancient** that you have seen or read about?

stratosphere • endow • charisma • ancient

Write on the board the four words studied this week. Read the words with the class and briefly review their meanings. Then conduct the oral activities below.

1 Tell students that you are going to give them a clue about one of the words for the week. They are to find the word that answers the clue.

- Most successful movie actors have this. **(charisma)**

- This word describes certain redwood trees. **(ancient)**

- This is one layer of Earth's atmosphere. **(the stratosphere)**

- Wealthy donors do this to charities and colleges. **(endow them with money or property)**

2 Read each sentence and ask students to supply the correct word to complete the sentence.

- Your parents' genes may ____ you with some of your talents. You acquire others on your own. **(endow)**

- On its way to the moon, the spacecraft entered the ____. **(stratosphere)**

- This TV show is not very entertaining, but its stars do have ____. **(charisma)**

- Native North Americans have lived on this continent since ____ times. **(ancient)**

3 Read each sentence and ask students to tell which word or words are wrong. Then have them provide the correct word from the week's list.

- The actor's repulsiveness earned him a starring role. **(repulsiveness/charisma)**

- These modern ruins are over a thousand years old. **(modern/ancient)**

- Alex is lucky that his parents purchased him a lot of musical talent. **(purchased him/endowed him with)**

4 Read each sentence and ask students to decide if it is true or false. If the sentence is false, instruct students to explain why.

- The stratosphere is about 50 miles thick. **(false; it is about 30 miles thick)**

- To endow an organization means to give it a gift of money or property. **(true)**

- World War II did not occur in ancient times. **(true)**

- *Charisma* and *appeal* are synonyms. **(true)**

Answers for page 83: 1. D, 2. H, 3. D, 4. G

Review Words	stratosphere • endow • charisma • ancient

Fill in the bubble next to the correct answer.

1. **Which word is an antonym for *ancient*?**
   - Ⓐ expensive
   - Ⓑ roomy
   - Ⓒ gorgeous
   - Ⓓ modern

2. **Which is true of someone with *charisma*?**
   - Ⓕ He or she is a brilliant student.
   - Ⓖ He or she is a gifted artist.
   - Ⓗ Most people like him or her.
   - Ⓙ He or she is a famous movie star.

3. **Where does the *stratosphere* begin?**
   - Ⓐ beneath Earth's surface
   - Ⓑ just above Earth's surface
   - Ⓒ in outer space
   - Ⓓ about 11 miles above Earth's surface

4. **How does someone *endow* a charity or other organization?**
   - Ⓕ by becoming a volunteer there
   - Ⓖ by giving the organization money
   - Ⓗ by naming the organization
   - Ⓙ by shutting down the organization

Writing

If you could travel back to ancient times, what place would you like to visit?
Use **ancient** in your sentences.

_____

_____

expose

verb

1. to make something known
2. to leave without protection

The detective **exposed** the professor as the mastermind of the plot. The invisible ink appeared when it was **exposed** to sunlight.

Which definition is being described: "to make something known" or "to leave without protection"?

- The journalist's investigation exposed several unsafe toys.
- A secret passage was exposed when the wall was removed.
- We were exposed to the harsh wind and rain when our tent blew away.
- I stayed home from school, not wanting to expose my classmates to my illness.
- The villain in the story seemed kind, but in the end, his evil deeds were exposed.

How do you avoid being **exposed** to too much sun?

distraction

noun

something that draws one's attention to it

The backyard party next door was a big **distraction** as I tried to concentrate on my homework.

Which of the following would be **distractions** for you when you do homework?

- loud music
- total silence
- the soft hum of a fan
- people talking quietly
- a band playing in the next room

How do you avoid **distractions** when working on something important?

luscious

adjective

smelling or
tasting delicious

The peach pie with vanilla ice cream was
a **luscious** dessert.

Complete this graphic organizer for **luscious**.

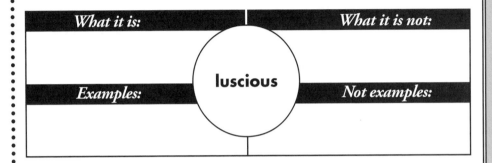

What it is:		What it is not:
	luscious	
Examples:		Not examples:

Give some examples of foods that you find **luscious**.

forfeit

verb

to give up the right
to something

We had to **forfeit** the soccer game because we
did not have enough players.

Which words have about the same meaning as **forfeit**?

- gain
- surrender
- acquire
- hand over
- relinquish

What are some other reasons you might **forfeit** a game?

expose • distraction • luscious • forfeit

Write on the board the four words studied this week. Read the words with the class and briefly review their meanings. Then conduct the oral activities below.

1 Tell students that you are going to give them a clue about one of the words for the week. They are to find the word that answers the clue.

- You might use this word to describe your favorite dessert. **(luscious)**

- You do this to your skin when you forget to use sunscreen on a sunny day. **(expose it to the sun)**

- Construction noise might be one if you are trying to read. **(a distraction)**

- A runner must do this if he or she breaks a rule during a race. **(forfeit the race)**

2 Read each sentence and ask students to supply the correct word to complete the sentence.

- Don't start a fight with your opponents, or you may have to ___ the game. **(forfeit)**

- I love the ___ smell of baking bread. **(luscious)**

- I promise not to ___ your secret to our friends. **(expose)**

- My dog kept barking, providing an annoying ___ as I tried to talk on the phone. **(distraction)**

3 Read each sentence and ask students to tell which word is wrong. Then have them provide the correct word from the week's list.

- I promised the magician not to conceal how he did the trick. **(conceal/expose)**

- Let's have these revolting strawberries for dessert. **(revolting/luscious)**

- You will win the competition if the judges notice that you're cheating. **(win/forfeit)**

4 Read each sentence and ask students to decide if it is true or false. If the sentence is false, instruct students to explain why.

- For some people, music does not act as a distraction. **(true)**

- Exposing your skin to the wind may dry it out. **(true)**

- When you forfeit a game, you lose it. **(true)**

- *Luscious* and *yummy* are antonyms. **(false; they are synonyms)**

Answers for page 87: 1. D, 2. H, 3. A, 4. G

Review Words expose • distraction • luscious • forfeit

Fill in the bubble next to the correct answer.

1. **Which word is a synonym for *luscious*?**
   - Ⓐ dry
   - Ⓑ bland
   - Ⓒ putrid
   - Ⓓ delicious

2. **When you are reading a book, which might be a *distraction*?**
   - Ⓕ the book's exciting plot
   - Ⓖ the book's interesting characters
   - Ⓗ a traffic accident outside your window
   - Ⓙ the comfortable chair you're sitting in

3. **Which word is a synonym for *expose*?**
   - Ⓐ reveal
   - Ⓑ conceal
   - Ⓒ analyze
   - Ⓓ pardon

4. **Why might a player have to *forfeit* a game?**
   - Ⓕ because he or she is winning
   - Ⓖ because he or she broke a rule
   - Ⓗ because he or she could lose
   - Ⓙ because he or she plays so well

Writing

Write about the most luscious dessert you can imagine. Use **luscious** in your sentences.

_____

_____

_____

ignorance

noun

a lack of knowledge

I decided to overcome my **ignorance** of computer programming and take a class.

Which word or words mean about the same as **ignorance**?

- complete understanding
- lack of awareness
- comprehension
- misinformation
- cluelessness

Have you ever heard the expression "**ignorance** is bliss"? What do you think the expression means? Do you agree with the expression?

vain

adjective

overly proud of one's looks, abilities, or accomplishments

antonym: humble

The **vain** actor kept photos of himself all over the house.

Complete this graphic organizer for **vain**.

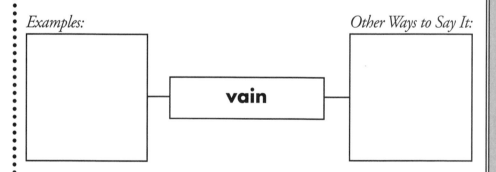

Examples: *Other Ways to Say It:*

vain

Do you think being **vain** is a positive or a negative quality? Why?

reunion

noun

the bringing together of friends, family, or other groups of people

Family members from all across the country got together at our **reunion**.

Which of these might happen at a **reunion**?

- exchanging e-mail addresses
- taking photographs
- doing homework
- sharing a meal
- playing games

Give examples of different groups of people that have **reunions**. Have you ever been to a **reunion**?

shallow

adjective

lacking deep thought, feeling, or knowledge

His **shallow** remarks about the book exposed his **shallow** understanding of the author's purpose.

If someone has a **shallow** personality, which of the following words might describe him or her?

- artificial
- sympathetic
- superficial
- insubstantial
- complex

Would a **shallow** person make a good friend? Why or why not?

---

ignorance • vain • reunion • shallow

Write on the board the four words studied this week. Read the words with the class and briefly review their meanings. Then conduct the oral activities below.

1 Tell students that you are going to give them a clue about one of the words for the week. They are to find the word that answers the clue.

- This word describes someone who looks in the mirror more often than necessary. **(vain)**

- This word describes a person who doesn't have deep feelings about things. **(shallow)**

- People can overcome this by reading a wide variety of books. **(ignorance)**

- This is an event at which people come together after being apart. **(a reunion)**

2 Read each sentence and ask students to supply the correct word to complete the sentence.

- Mom saw many former classmates at her college ＿＿＿. **(reunion)**

- I'm proud of my artistic talent, but I don't think I'm ＿＿＿ about it. **(vain)**

- Ben's ＿＿＿ of current TV shows is due to the fact that he rarely watches TV. **(ignorance)**

- A doctor's knowledge of diseases should not be ＿＿＿. **(shallow)**

3 Read each sentence and ask students to tell which word is wrong. Then have them provide the correct word from the week's list.

- Ken revealed his mastery of algebra by failing the algebra test. **(mastery/ignorance)**

- A college professor's knowledge of subject matter should not be deep. **(deep/shallow)**

- Liz is so humble that she won't stop bragging about her athletic triumphs. **(humble/vain)**

- After ten years of not performing together, we were thrilled to hear about the band's scheduled breakup concert. **(breakup/reunion)**

4 Read each sentence and ask students to decide if it is true or false. If the sentence is false, instruct students to explain why.

- At a reunion, everyone meets each other for the first time. **(false; they meet again)**

- *Ignorance* and *knowledge* are not the same thing. **(true)**

- If you comprehend the meaning of a poem, you have a shallow understanding. **(false; you have a deep understanding)**

- All pretty women are vain about their looks. **(false; some don't give their appearance much thought)**

Answers for page 91: 1. D, 2. G, 3. A, 4. H

Name _____

Fill in the bubble next to the correct answer.

1. **Which pair of words are synonyms for *shallow*?**
   - Ⓐ silly, serious
   - Ⓑ casual, enduring
   - Ⓒ deep, complicated
   - Ⓓ superficial, trivial

2. **Which describes a family *reunion*?**
   - Ⓕ a photograph of a large family
   - Ⓖ a gathering for many family members
   - Ⓗ a home that the owner inherited from a family member
   - Ⓙ a married couple's children and grandchildren

3. **Which word is an antonym for *vain*?**
   - Ⓐ humble
   - Ⓑ humorous
   - Ⓒ selfish
   - Ⓓ conceited

4. **Which sentence reveals *ignorance* about geometry?**
   - Ⓕ If you find the number of square feet in a room, you have found the area.
   - Ⓖ Streets that are parallel point in the same direction.
   - Ⓗ A stop sign has a triangular shape.
   - Ⓙ The distance around the playground is its perimeter.

Writing

Write about a topic or subject that you would like to know about. Use **ignorance** in your sentences.

_____

_____

_____

akimbo

adjective

with hands on hips and elbows turned outward

When my mother stands with her arms **akimbo**, I know she means business.

What might a person's body language be saying if he or she were standing with arms **akimbo**?

- I'm irritated.
- I'm watching intently.
- I'm feeling silly.
- I'm frustrated.
- I'm sad.

Try standing with your arms **akimbo**. How does that posture make you feel?

banish

verb

to punish someone by making him or her permanently leave a country

The king **banished** the knight for betraying his master.

Which of these mean about the same as **banish**?

- to welcome home
- to greet warmly
- to send away
- to cast out
- to run out

Why do you think someone would be **banished**? Who can be **banished**? Who can **banish** others?

ignorance • vain • reunion • shallow

A Word a Day • EMC 2796 • © Evan-Moor Corp.

calligraphy

noun

a style of beautiful or elegant handwriting

The invitations were painstakingly hand-lettered in elegant **calligraphy**.

Which of the following might you need if you wanted to learn **calligraphy**?

- special pens
- ink
- patience
- crayons
- a steady hand

Have you seen **calligraphy**? Tell about where you saw it and what words were written.

essential

adjective

very important or necessary

Sugar is an **essential** ingredient in making sugar cookies.

Complete this graphic organizer for **essential**.

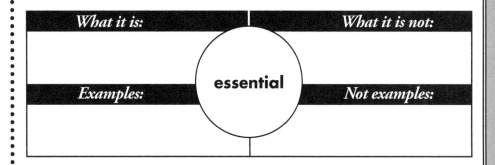

What are some **essential** ingredients for making vegetable soup?

akimbo • banish • calligraphy • essential

Write on the board the four words studied this week. Read the words with the class and briefly review their meanings. Then conduct the oral activities below.

1 Tell students that you are going to give them a clue about one of the words for the week. They are to find the word that answers the clue.

- This word describes a recipe ingredient that you cannot do without. (**essential**)

- This is an artistic type of handwriting. (**calligraphy**)

- Someone who stands with his or her arms this way might be mad at you. (**akimbo**)

- A ruler might do this to an enemy. (**banish him or her**)

2 Read each sentence and ask students to supply the correct word to complete the sentence.

- "Be careful," said the princess, "or my father may ____ you from his kingdom." (**banish**)

- Expanding your vocabulary is an ____ part of improving your reading skills. (**essential**)

- The coach stood on the sidelines with arms ____ as he watched his team fail to make a first down. (**akimbo**)

- Alexa needs a special pen and a bottle of ink so she can practice ____. (**calligraphy**)

3 Read each sentence and ask students to tell which word is wrong. Then have them provide the correct word from the week's list.

- Kara addressed her party invitations in elegant scribbling. (**scribbling/calligraphy**)

- British judges used to welcome criminals to Australia. (**welcome/banish**)

- Eggs are an optional ingredient in an omelet recipe. (**optional/essential**)

4 Read each sentence and ask students to decide if it is true or false. If the sentence is false, instruct students to explain why.

- People don't stand with their legs akimbo. (**true**)

- To banish someone is to invite the person in. (**false; banishment means to send away**)

- *Essential* and *trivial* are antonyms. (**true**)

- Some people consider calligraphy an art form. (**true**)

Answers for page 95: 1. B, 2. J, 3. D, 4. H

Review Words   akimbo • banish • calligraphy • essential

Fill in the bubble next to the correct answer.

1. **Which word is an antonym for *essential*?**
   Ⓐ undivided
   Ⓑ unnecessary
   Ⓒ unsatisfied
   Ⓓ unstoppable

2. **When would someone be most likely to use *calligraphy*?**
   Ⓕ when solving a series of math problems on a test
   Ⓖ when scribbling a quick message to a family member
   Ⓗ when typing a long e-mail to a friend in another city
   Ⓙ when addressing envelopes for wedding invitations

3. **Who is most likely to stand with arms *akimbo*?**
   Ⓐ someone who is waving to someone else
   Ⓑ someone who is about to hug someone else
   Ⓒ someone who feels frightened
   Ⓓ someone who feels irritated

4. **Which word is an antonym for *banish*?**
   Ⓕ scrutinize
   Ⓖ exclude
   Ⓗ welcome
   Ⓙ dismiss

Writing

Write about a time when you saw someone stand with his or her arms akimbo.
Tell what happened. Use **akimbo** in your sentences.

_____

_____

_____

formidable

adjective

exceptionally difficult or fearsome

The heavyweight boxer had not lost a bout and was considered a **formidable** opponent.

Complete this graphic organizer for **formidable**.

Examples:

Other Ways to Say It:

formidable

What is something that seems **formidable** to you? Why?

esophagus

noun

the tube that carries food from the throat to the stomach

The human **esophagus** is about nine inches long.

Which of these body parts work with the **esophagus**?

- the foot
- the neck
- the mouth
- the kneecap
- the stomach

Touch your neck and feel where your **esophagus** is located.

sanction

verb

to give approval

The school board **sanctioned** the building of a new middle school.

Which words mean about the same as **sanction**?

- authorize
- support
- permit
- reject
- deny

Would you **sanction** a decision to have school on Saturdays?

pharmacist

noun

a person trained to prepare and give out medicines

The **pharmacist** filled my prescription and made sure I understood the instructions for taking the medication.

Which of these might a **pharmacist** do?

- count out pills
- use a computer
- take customers' orders
- help customers try on shoes
- tell customers about medication side effects

What might be difficult about being a **pharmacist**?
What might be enjoyable about it?

formidable • esophagus • sanction • pharmacist

Write on the board the four words studied this week. Read the words with the class and briefly review their meanings. Then conduct the oral activities below.

1 Tell students that you are going to give them a clue about one of the words for the week. They are to find the word that answers the clue.

- You use this body part to swallow your food. **(esophagus)**

- This person fills doctors' prescriptions. **(a pharmacist)**

- When you do this, you say that something is okay with you. **(sanction it)**

- This word describes strong opponents or enemies. **(formidable)**

2 Read each sentence and ask students to supply the correct word to complete the sentence.

- I can't ____ cruelty by pretending not to notice it, so I always report bullying to school authorities. **(sanction)**

- My doctor called the ____ and asked her to give me an antibiotic. **(pharmacist)**

- Food travels down your ____ to your stomach. **(esophagus)**

- Climbing Mount Everest is a ____ undertaking. **(formidable)**

3 Read each sentence and ask students to tell which word or words are wrong. Then have them provide the correct word from the week's list.

- We felt certain the principal would forbid our plan to raise money for the library. **(forbid/sanction)**

- Food travels down your nasal passages to your belly. **(nasal passages/esophagus)**

- Taylor is a weak competitor who rarely loses. **(weak/formidable)**

4 Read each sentence and ask students to decide if it is true or false. If the sentence is false, instruct students to explain why.

- Pharmacists prescribe medicines. **(false; they fill prescriptions; doctors prescribe medicines)**

- Most cultures sanction murder. **(false; the opposite is true)**

- *Formidable* and *frail* are antonyms. **(true)**

- Your esophagus connects your throat and stomach. **(true)**

Answers for page 99: 1. A, 2. H, 3. C, 4. J

| **Review Words** | formidable • esophagus • sanction • pharmacist |

Fill in the bubble next to the correct answer.

1. **Which word is an antonym for *sanction*?**
   - Ⓐ forbid
   - Ⓑ foretell
   - Ⓒ foresee
   - Ⓓ forgive

2. **How does a *pharmacist* help medical patients?**
   - Ⓕ by diagnosing illnesses
   - Ⓖ by performing surgery
   - Ⓗ by distributing medicines
   - Ⓙ by administering blood tests

3. **Where is a person's *esophagus* located?**
   - Ⓐ in the person's stomach and intestines
   - Ⓑ in the person's eyes and nose
   - Ⓒ in the person's neck and chest
   - Ⓓ in the person's brain

4. **Which word is an antonym for *formidable*?**
   - Ⓕ intelligent
   - Ⓖ sneaky
   - Ⓗ mighty
   - Ⓙ weak

Writing

Write about something you wish school officials would sanction. Use **sanction** in your sentences.

_____

_____

_____

limber

adjective

bending easily

synonym: flexible

Gymnasts must be strong and **limber** to do all those flips and jumps.

Complete this graphic organizer for **limber**.

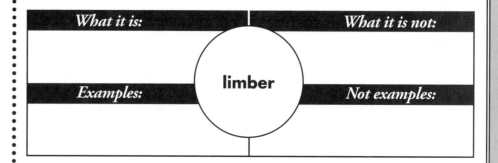

What is something you can do that requires you to be **limber**?

campaign

noun

a series of planned activities to bring about a desired result

The women's club staged a **campaign** to convince the city council to refurbish the homeless shelter.

Which words mean about the same as **campaign**?

- push
- mission
- effort
- retreat
- movement

Name some other types of **campaigns** you know about.

majestic

adjective

grand or spectacular

antonym: inferior

As we left the lowlands, **majestic**, snowcapped mountains rose up in the distance.

Which words mean about the same as **majestic**?

- breathtaking
- magnificent
- average
- splendid
- humble

Mention some other natural wonders that you think are **majestic**.

concoct

verb

1. to prepare by mixing several different things together; to combine

2. to make up something untruthful

I love to **concoct** smoothies with frozen fruit, yogurt, and juice.

Which meaning is being used: "to combine" or "to invent an untruth"?

- Let's concoct a totally awesome sandwich.
- Famous chefs concoct new recipes all the time.
- She concocted an excuse for not having done her report.
- My brother concocts incredible stories to get out of trouble when he is late.
- He concocted an elaborate dessert for the dinner party.

Give some examples of things you or your family **concoct**.

limber • campaign • majestic • concoct

Write on the board the four words studied this week. Read the words with the class and briefly review their meanings. Then conduct the oral activities below.

1 Tell students that you are going to give them a clue about one of the words for the week. They are to find the word that answers the clue.

- You might use this word to describe the Grand Canyon. **(majestic)**

- You might use this word to describe an acrobat. **(limber)**

- Every political candidate has one. Its purpose is to get him or her elected. **(a campaign)**

- You do this when you combine ingredients to prepare something. **(concoct)**

2 Read each sentence and ask students to supply the correct word to complete the sentence.

- To ___ salsa, Dad chops and mixes onions, garlic, tomatoes, chilies, and herbs. **(concoct)**

- A ___ redwood tree towered above the lodge. **(majestic)**

- A ballet dancer must stretch every day to stay ___. **(limber)**

- The advertising firm launched a television ad ___ to sell the new toothpaste. **(campaign)**

3 Read each list of words and phrases. Ask students to supply the word that fits best with each.

- magnificent, grand, spectacular, breathtaking **(majestic)**

- gymnast, ballet dancer, graceful, flexible **(limber)**

- political, fundraising, advertising **(campaign)**

- combine, blend, mix together, fake, falsify **(concoct)**

4 Read each sentence and ask students to decide if it is true or false. If the sentence is false, instruct students to explain why.

- Stretching regularly can keep your body limber. **(true)**

- If you concoct an excuse, you make it up. **(true)**

- *Majestic* and *unremarkable* are antonyms. **(true)**

- A political campaign is a person who is running for office. **(false; candidates run for office; a political campaign is a plan to win)**

Answers for page 103: 1. D, 2. G, 3. D, 4. G

Review Words limber • campaign • majestic • concoct

Fill in the bubble next to the correct answer.

1. **Which pair of words are synonyms for *concoct*?**
   - Ⓐ preheat, create
   - Ⓑ presume, brew
   - Ⓒ predate, fabricate
   - Ⓓ prepare, invent

2. **Which word is a synonym for *majestic*?**
   - Ⓕ bossy
   - Ⓖ grand
   - Ⓗ wealthy
   - Ⓙ stylish

3. **Which sentence accurately describes a political *campaign*?**
   - Ⓐ He or she is an elected government official.
   - Ⓑ It is an office such as a senate seat or the U.S. presidency.
   - Ⓒ He or she is a voter who elects candidates to political office.
   - Ⓓ It is a series of activities aimed at getting someone elected.

4. **Which sentence does not use the word *limber* correctly?**
   - Ⓕ Mom takes a yoga class to help her stay limber.
   - Ⓖ I limber up the stairs when I have a loaded backpack.
   - Ⓗ One needs to be limber in order to do acrobatics.
   - Ⓙ In general, children are more limber than their grandparents.

Writing

Write about the most majestic sight you have ever seen. Use **majestic** in your sentences.

_____

_____

_____

ballyhoo

noun

a noisy disturbance; an uproar

There was a big **ballyhoo** as the home team took the field.

Which words have about the same meaning as **ballyhoo**?

- commotion
- racket
- quietude
- hullabaloo
- tranquility

Where have you heard a **ballyhoo**?

mischievous

adjective

playful and mildly naughty

The **mischievous** puppy chewed on all my shoes.

Which words mean about the same as **mischievous**?

- kind
- impish
- devilish
- obedient
- thoughtful

Describe a time when you were **mischievous**.

enunciate

verb

to pronounce words, especially in a clear voice

Our teacher **enunciates** so that students who are learning English can understand her.

Complete this graphic organizer for **enunciate**.

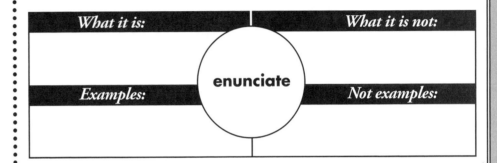

Think of a sentence to say out loud. **Enunciate** as you say each word.

intimate

adjective

close and familiar

My mother has been **intimate** friends with Mrs. Mendez since they were in high school.

Which words have about the same meaning as **intimate**?

- warm
- affectionate
- chummy
- distant
- dear

What qualities do you look for in an **intimate** friend? Why is it important to have a few **intimate** friends?

ballyhoo • mischievous • enunciate • intimate

Write on the board the four words studied this week. Read the words with the class and briefly review their meanings. Then conduct the oral activities below.

1 Tell students that you are going to give them a clue about one of the words for the week. They are to find the word that answers the clue.

- You might use this word to describe a child who is always getting into things. (**mischievous**)

- You might use this word to describe your relationship with your best friend. (**intimate**)

- People should do this when they give speeches. (**enunciate**)

- You might hear one at a campaign rally. (**a ballyhoo**)

2 Read each sentence and ask students to supply the correct word to complete the sentence.

- That ____ kitten has stolen my sock! (**mischievous**)

- Ms. Lee and Ms. Murphy have been ____ friends since they were children. (**intimate**)

- Try to ____ so I can understand what you're saying. (**enunciate**)

- On New Year's Eve there was a ____ in the town square as the clock struck midnight. (**ballyhoo**)

3 Read each sentence and ask students to tell which word is wrong. Then have them provide the correct word from the week's list.

- The twins are always together and have a very impersonal relationship. (**impersonal/intimate**)

- It is important to mumble when you give an oral report. (**mumble/enunciate**)

- That well-behaved child has tied my shoelaces together again. (**well-behaved/mischievous**)

- We couldn't sleep on New Year's Eve because of the calmness next door. (**calmness/ballyhoo**)

4 Read each sentence and ask students to decide if it is true or false. If the sentence is false, instruct students to explain why.

- You might hear a ballyhoo at a high school pep rally. (**true**)

- Some people think mischievous behavior is cute. (**true**)

- *Intimate* and *affectionate* are synonyms. (**true**)

- Good speakers never enunciate. (**false; good speakers speak clearly**)

Answers for page 107: 1. C, 2. H, 3. A, 4. J

Name _____

Fill in the bubble next to the correct answer.

1. **Which word is an antonym for *enunciate*?**
   - Ⓐ glimpse
   - Ⓑ stare
   - Ⓒ mumble
   - Ⓓ shout

2. **Which word is a synonym for *mischievous*?**
   - Ⓕ snobbish
   - Ⓖ cautious
   - Ⓗ playful
   - Ⓙ obedient

3. **Which set of adjectives best describe a *ballyhoo*?**
   - Ⓐ loud, enthusiastic, noisy, showy
   - Ⓑ calm, quiet, soothing, restful, peaceful
   - Ⓒ babyish, childish, silly, juvenile, immature
   - Ⓓ serious, important, stern, official, strict

4. **In which sentence could *intimate* be used to fill in the blank?**
   - Ⓕ Appendicitis can result in ____ pain.
   - Ⓖ The ____ designs on the silk fabric must have taken hours to weave.
   - Ⓗ Parrots often ____ words that their owners make.
   - Ⓙ I whisper when I want to share a secret with an ____ friend.

Writing

Write about the behavior of a mischievous child or book character whom you know of or about. Use **mischievous** in your sentences.

_____

_____

_____

concise

adjective

expressed in a few words

synonym: brief

Isaac's report was **concise** yet packed with information.

Complete this graphic organizer for **concise**.

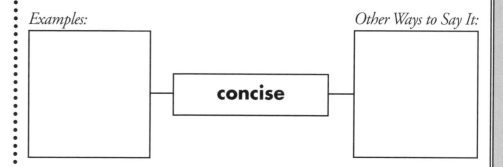

Examples:

concise

Other Ways to Say It:

Give examples of some things you've read that are both informative and **concise**.

banter

noun

playful, teasing conversation

synonym: repartee

At the end of each newscast, the news anchor and the sportscaster like to engage in **banter** about the local baseball team's performance.

Which words mean about the same as **banter**?

- ribbing
- jesting
- ignoring
- heckling
- kidding

Where might you hear **banter** between people?

gesture

noun

a movement of the hands or head that has meaning

verb

to move your hands or head to emphasize what you are saying or thinking

An international **gesture** meaning "silence" is an index finger pressed to the lips.
People from some cultures **gesture** more than others when they speak.

Which definition is being used: "a meaningful movement" or "to move your hands or head when speaking"?

- The librarian gestured for us to sit down on the carpet.
- Sam gives great presentations because his hand gestures emphasize what he's saying.
- Ms. Mills is gesturing for us to come where she is.
- My grandmother gestures a lot when she talks.
- I taught my dog a gesture that means "lie down."

What are some **gestures** that have definite meanings?

aquatic

adjective

in water or taking place in water

The **aquatic** plants lent a lush look to our fish tank.

Which of the following are **aquatic** sports?

- snorkeling
- hockey
- diving
- windsurfing
- ping-pong

Name some **aquatic** plants or creatures.

concise • banter • gesture • aquatic

Write on the board the four words studied this week. Read the words with the class and briefly review their meanings. Then conduct the oral activities below.

1 Tell students that you are going to give them a clue about one of the words for the week. They are to find the word that answers the clue.

- This word describes plants such as seaweed. **(aquatic)**

- You might use this word to describe a short, informative speech. **(concise)**

- Almost all speakers do this during their speeches. **(gesture)**

- You may hear this between friends on the school bus. **(banter)**

2 Read each sentence and ask students to supply the correct word to complete the sentence.

- At a party, it helps to be good at ____. **(banter)**

- Give a ____ oral report of five minutes or less. **(concise)**

- Frogs are ____ creatures, but they spend part of their lives on land, as well. **(aquatic)**

- Nodding your head is a ____ that usually means "yes." **(gesture)**

3 Read each sentence and ask students to tell which word or words are wrong. Then have them provide the correct word from the week's list.

- Please write a lengthy statement of three sentences or less. **(lengthy/concise)**

- Climate change affects land animals such as whales and dolphins. **(land/aquatic)**

- Speakers of many languages often remain motionless in order to communicate. **(remain motionless/gesture)**

- The jovial adults engaged in serious conversation while the children were playing in the pool. **(serious conversation/banter)**

4 Read each sentence and ask students to decide if it is true or false. If the sentence is false, instruct students to explain why.

- Gestures help people to communicate. **(true)**

- Chatty people prefer concise phone conversations. **(false; they like long conversations)**

- *Banter* and *jesting* are synonyms. **(true)**

- *Aquatic* and *marine* are synonyms. **(true)**

Answers for page 111: 1. C, 2. J, 3. B, 4. J

Name _____

Fill in the bubble next to the correct answer.

1. **Which word is a synonym for *banter*?**
   Ⓐ scolding
   Ⓑ explaining
   Ⓒ teasing
   Ⓓ lecturing

2. **Which word is an antonym for *concise*?**
   Ⓕ clear
   Ⓖ brief
   Ⓗ precise
   Ⓙ lengthy

3. **What do people use to *gesture* as they speak?**
   Ⓐ their ears and noses
   Ⓑ their heads and hands
   Ⓒ their legs and feet
   Ⓓ their hearts and lungs

4. **Which sentence uses the word *aquatic* correctly?**
   Ⓕ He is an avid aquatic who knows a lot about fish.
   Ⓖ Aquatic is my favorite shade of blue.
   Ⓗ The ancient Romans built a large aquatic to carry water to Rome.
   Ⓙ This nursery specializes in aquatic plants for ponds.

Writing

Write about an aquatic creature that interests you. Use **aquatic** in your sentences.

_____

_____

_____

enthrall

verb

to hold one's interest completely

synonym: to entrance

I was **enthralled** by the book and read nonstop for hours.

Which words have about the same meaning as **enthrall**?

- tire
- bore
- enchant
- captivate
- mesmerize

What types of activities **enthrall** you?

dignity

noun

a manner or quality that makes a person worthy of respect

Even though the actor momentarily forgot his lines, he managed to pick up and continue with **dignity**.

Which of these people display **dignity**?

- a bully who picks fights
- a teacher who is always fair-minded
- a politician who does not put down his opponents
- a driver who honks and yells at other drivers
- a rock star whose public actions are always courteous

Can you name any public figures who display **dignity**?

buoyant

adjective

1. capable of floating

2. having a lighthearted, cheerful nature

The inner tube was **buoyant** enough to support three people.

Which meaning does each example illustrate: "able to float" or "cheerful"?

- an apple bobbing in a tub of water
- a life vest
- a bouncy personality
- a swimming pool float
- an enthusiastic greeting

Give an example of something **buoyant**.

murmur

verb

to say words in a soft voice

It's OK to talk in the library if you **murmur**.

Complete this graphic organizer for **murmur**.

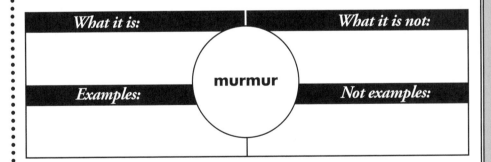

What it is:			*What it is not:*
	murmur		
Examples:			*Not examples:*

Besides a library, in what other places might it be best to **murmur**?

enthrall • dignity • buoyant • murmur

Write on the board the four words studied this week. Read the words with the class and briefly review their meanings. Then conduct the oral activities below.

1 Tell students that you are going to give them a clue about one of the words for the week. They are to find the word that answers the clue.

- This word describes rafts and rowboats. **(buoyant)**

- A gifted entertainer does this to the audience members. **(enthralls them)**

- You might do this if you were telling a secret. **(murmur)**

- People who are sure of themselves may display this quality in public. **(dignity)**

2 Read each sentence and ask students to supply the correct word to complete the sentence.

- Even though she came in second, Taylor displayed great ____ as she congratulated the winner. **(dignity)**

- Skilled magicians can ____ their audiences. **(enthrall)**

- I don't like it when other moviegoers ____ to each other during the show. **(murmur)**

- An empty glass bottle is ____ enough to float if you cork it tightly. **(buoyant)**

3 Read each sentence and ask students to tell which word or words are wrong. Then have them provide the correct word from the week's list.

- Actors hope to bore their audiences. **(bore/enthrall)**

- Driftwood is heavy enough to float. **(heavy/buoyant)**

- The team received a sportsmanship award for maintaining their bad manners at all times. **(bad manners/dignity)**

- Please shout so you won't wake the baby. **(shout/murmur)**

4 Read each sentence and ask students to decide if it is true or false. If the sentence is false, instruct students to explain why.

- Murmuring is similar to whispering. **(true)**

- Metal canoes and kayaks can be buoyant. **(true)**

- *Enthrall* and *mesmerize* are synonyms. **(true)**

- *Dignity* and *shame* are synonyms. **(false; they are antonyms)**

Answers for page 115: 1. C, 2. J, 3. C, 4. F

Name _____

Fill in the bubble next to the correct answer.

1. Which word is an antonym for *murmur*?

Ⓐ whisper

Ⓑ reveal

Ⓒ shout

Ⓓ conceal

2. Which word is a synonym for *dignity*?

Ⓕ vanity

Ⓖ shyness

Ⓗ selfishness

Ⓙ self-confidence

3. Which of these is most *buoyant*?

Ⓐ a boulder

Ⓑ a coin

Ⓒ a canoe

Ⓓ a pebble

4. Which word could be used instead of *enthrall* in this sentence?

Films that explore nature, whether in rainforests or deserts, absolutely <u>enthrall</u> me.

Ⓕ mesmerize

Ⓖ entertain

Ⓗ bore

Ⓙ interest

Writing

Write about a time when someone you know displayed dignity. Use **dignity** in your sentences.

_____

_____

_____

endeavor

noun

a serious attempt to do something

verb

to make an effort

He was successful in his **endeavor** to get A's in his science classes. His plan is to **endeavor** to become a scientist.

Which definition is being used: "a serious attempt" or "to make an effort"?

- Rosa and Mateo endeavor to finish all their homework before dinner.
- Her endeavor to win the National Spelling Bee met with success.
- Maxine's endeavor to start a video game company is very ambitious.
- Jane endeavored to finish the 900-page novel in one day.
- Villains in stories endeavor to overpower the heroes.

Name some of your **endeavors**.

triumph

verb

to obtain a great success or victory

The gymnast **triumphed** in the competition and won an Olympic gold medal.

Complete this graphic organizer for **triumph**.

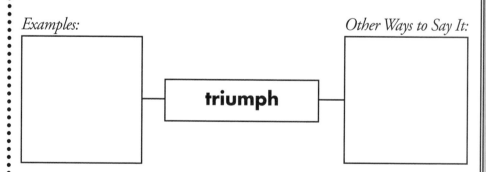

Examples: *Other Ways to Say It:*

triumph

Give an example of one of your personal **triumphs**.

circumstance

noun

a fact connected with a particular event, such as time, location, and other specifics

The heat and lack of air conditioning made for very difficult test-taking **circumstances**.

Which words mean about the same as **circumstance**?

- condition
- situation
- feelings
- experiment
- factor

Describe the **circumstances** of how you first met someone you know.

juvenile

adjective

1. not mature; young
2. immature in actions; childish

The marathon organizer gave a special prize for **juvenile** runners.

Which meaning is being used: "young" or "childish"?

- Sometimes your juvenile behavior is embarrassing!
- I won't even respond to such a juvenile remark!
- We rescued a juvenile hawk that had a broken wing.
- A juvenile turkey is called a poult.
- To argue over who gets to sit in the recliner is juvenile.

At what age do you think people should no longer act **juvenile**?

endeavor • triumph • circumstance • juvenile

Write on the board the four words studied this week. Read the words with the class and briefly review their meanings. Then conduct the oral activities below.

1 Tell students that you are going to give them a clue about one of the words for the week. They are to find the word that answers the clue.

- This word describes someone or something not yet adult. **(juvenile)**

- Sports teams do this when they win by large margins. **(triumph)**

- This is a condition that may affect an outcome. **(a circumstance)**

- You do this when you make an attempt to do something. **(endeavor)**

2 Read each sentence and ask students to supply the correct word to complete the sentence.

- Under other ____, I wouldn't excuse your tardiness, but the bus breaking down is an acceptable excuse. **(circumstances)**

- My ____ to break the world record for time spent playing tiddlywinks has been unsuccessful so far, but I'll keep trying. **(endeavor)**

- ____ lawbreakers and those over 18 are usually tried in different courts. **(Juvenile)**

- I'm absolutely positive that our team will ____ in the state semifinals. **(triumph)**

3 Read each sentence and ask students to tell which word or words are wrong. Then have them provide the correct word from the week's list.

- Winners usually fail due to perseverance and skill. **(fail/triumph)**

- Mr. Stone is one middle school teacher who won't tolerate mature behavior in class. **(mature/juvenile)**

- When I make a promise, I never try to keep it. **(never try/endeavor)**

4 Read each sentence and ask students to decide if it is true or false. If the sentence is false, instruct students to explain why.

- Circumstances rarely excuse misbehavior. **(true)**

- When there is a tie game, one team triumphs. **(false; neither team wins a victory)**

- *Juvenile* and *adolescent* are synonyms. **(true)**

- *Endeavor, attempt,* and *try* are all synonyms. **(true)**

Answers for page 119: 1. D, 2. H, 3. C, 4. J

Name _____

Review Words   endeavor • triumph • circumstance • juvenile

Fill in the bubble next to the correct answer.

1. **Which word is an antonym for *triumph*?**
   Ⓐ toil
   Ⓑ frolic
   Ⓒ win
   Ⓓ lose

2. **Which word is a synonym for *circumstance*?**
   Ⓕ conception
   Ⓖ confusion
   Ⓗ condition
   Ⓙ conclusion

3. **Which of these sentences does not describe *juvenile* behavior?**
   Ⓐ The professional basketball player got mad and stomped off the court.
   Ⓑ When we cut in front of that car, the driver stuck out his tongue at us.
   Ⓒ The clerk at the shoe store waited patiently while I tried on twelve pairs of sandals.
   Ⓓ Whenever he's not winning at checkers, Greg tips over the board.

4. **Which of these would not require much of an *endeavor*?**
   Ⓕ writing a successful novel
   Ⓖ reading the whole encyclopedia
   Ⓗ learning to play the guitar
   Ⓙ tying your shoes

Writing

Is it ever appropriate to act in a juvenile manner? Explain. Use **juvenile** in your sentences.

_____

_____

_____

irresistible

adjective

impossible to resist

The fuzzy stuffed dog was so **irresistible** that I just had to buy it.

Complete this graphic organizer for **irresistible**.

Examples: *Other Ways to Say It:*

irresistible

What is something you find **irresistible**?

compel

verb

to force to some action

The student's mischievous behavior throughout the assembly **compelled** the principal to send him to the office.

Which words mean about the same as **compel**?

- encourage
- require
- urge
- ignore
- pressure

Who **compels** you to do your best? How does he or she **compel** you?

enlist

verb

1. to get the help or support of

2. to join the armed forces

Can we **enlist** your help in collecting cellphones? We want to send them to soldiers who **enlist** in the army and are sent overseas.

Which meaning is being used: "to join" or "to get someone's help"?

- Some people enlist in the army to receive career training.
- Animal rights groups often enlist the support of celebrities to draw more attention to their causes.
- To get ready for the block party, we will need to enlist the help of the whole neighborhood.
- Soon after she enlisted, Rachel went off to basic training.
- The article in the newspaper said the aquarium needs to enlist more volunteers.

Who can you **enlist** to help you with your homework?

authentic

adjective

the real thing

antonym: imitation

This store sells **authentic** Native American jewelry and baskets.

Which words mean about the same as **authentic**?

- legitimate
- genuine
- phony
- false
- fake

Do you own something that is **authentic**? Describe it.

irresistible • compel • enlist • authentic

Write on the board the four words studied this week. Read the words with the class and briefly review their meanings. Then conduct the oral activities below.

1 Tell students that you are going to give them a clue about one of the words for the week. They are to find the word that answers the clue.

- This word describes something real, such as fur. **(authentic)**

- A guilty feeling can do this when it forces you to apologize. **(compel you)**

- You might use this word to describe an urge to buy something that you want very, very much. **(irresistible)**

- People do this when they join the U.S. Army. **(enlist)**

2 Read each sentence and ask students to supply the correct word to complete the sentence.

- Whom can I ____ to help me prepare dinner? **(enlist)**

- Ms. Asher doesn't believe in wearing ____ fur clothing, so she has a fake fur jacket. **(authentic)**

- Sometimes my urge to giggle in class becomes ____ and I'm forced to give in to it. **(irresistible)**

- Your conscience may ____ you to do the right thing, even when you think it would be easier to act otherwise. **(compel)**

3 Read each sentence and ask students to tell which word or words are wrong. Then have them provide the correct word from the week's list.

- I'm full, but I must have a slice of your repulsive homemade pie. **(repulsive/irresistible)**

- President George Washington signed this fake document. **(fake/authentic)**

- As soon as she turns 18, Chloe plans to leave the navy. **(leave/enlist in)**

- Your rude actions coax me to take disciplinary steps. **(coax/compel)**

4 Read each sentence and ask students to decide if it is true or false. If the sentence is false, instruct students to explain why.

- When you are famished, cooking smells can be irresistible. **(true)**

- Children may enlist in the U.S. Armed Forces. **(false; only people over 18 may enlist)**

- *Compel* and *drive* are synonyms. **(true)**

- *Authentic, genuine,* and *real* are all synonyms. **(true)**

Answers for page 123: 1. D, 2. G, 3. C, 4. H

Review Words	irresistible • compel • enlist • authentic

Fill in the bubble next to the correct answer.

1. Which word is an antonym for *authentic*?

Ⓐ fancy

Ⓑ old-fashioned

Ⓒ expensive

Ⓓ fake

2. Which words are synonyms for *compel*?

Ⓕ invite, welcome, beckon

Ⓖ force, require, make, urge

Ⓗ ask, plead, beg, wheedle

Ⓙ detain, arrest, imprison

3. Which sentence does not use the word *enlist* correctly?

Ⓐ We hope to enlist Dad to fix our computer.

Ⓑ Would you rather enlist in the navy or the air force?

Ⓒ I enlist that you stop arguing immediately.

Ⓓ The animal shelter needs to enlist help to groom animals.

4. In which sentence could *irresistible* be used to fill in the blank?

Ⓕ Air is ____ and can't be seen.

Ⓖ We can't turn back once we've made this ____ decision.

Ⓗ I find any dessert made of chocolate to be ____.

Ⓙ I think your fear of spiders is ____.

Writing

Write about a food that you find irresistible. Use **irresistible** in your sentences.

_____

_____

_____

nerve

noun

1. a bundle of fibers connecting the brain and parts of the body
2. courage or bravery

Every **nerve** in my body was on edge until the firefighter came out safely. He had a lot of **nerve** to run into the burning building.

Which definition is being used: "bundle of fibers that carry information from and to the brain" or "courage or bravery"?

- You've got some nerve talking to the teacher like that!
- Bungee jumping requires more nerve than I have!
- The surgeon endeavored to repair the damaged nerve.
- Each nerve in my body tingled with anticipation as I waited my turn to perform.
- Let me take a few deep breaths and get my nerve up.

What is something daring that you have had the **nerve** to try?

influential

adjective

being able to change or affect someone or something

A very **influential** music teacher convinced me to continue studying the cello.

Complete this graphic organizer for **influential**.

Examples: *Other Ways to Say It:*

influential

Who is the most **influential** person in your life? Tell why.

patronize

verb

to regularly shop at or use the services of

synonym:
to frequent

My parents prefer to **patronize** the locally owned market instead of the national chain.

Which of these could you **patronize**?

- a bakery
- a hair salon
- your friend's house
- a gas station
- a dry cleaner

What businesses do you and your family **patronize**?

galaxy

noun

1. a group of brilliant, beautiful, or famous people

2. a large group of stars and planets, and other matter

A **galaxy** of notable astronomers gathered to discuss the recent photographs of the Andromeda **Galaxy**.

Which meaning is being used: "a group of stars and planets" or "a group of notable people"?

- A galaxy of stars turned out for the film awards.
- Earth is in the Milky Way galaxy.
- The Hubble Space Telescope has taken photos of faraway galaxies.
- The political convention was attended by a galaxy of influential people.
- A galaxy of world-class athletes gathered for the opening ceremony of the Olympics.

Tell something you know about the **galaxy** we live in.

nerve • influential • patronize • galaxy

Write on the board the four words studied this week. Read the words with the class and briefly review their meanings. Then conduct the oral activities below.

1 Tell students that you are going to give them a clue about one of the words for the week. They are to find the word that answers the clue.

- Our solar system is part of one. **(a galaxy)**

- This word describes people who are powerful enough to convince others to do something. **(influential)**

- You do this when you shop at a certain store. **(patronize it)**

- These body parts detect heat, cold, and pain. **(nerves)**

2 Read each sentence and ask students to supply the correct word to complete the sentence.

- Mom's college English professor was ____ in her life. He urged her to become a professional writer. **(influential)**

- My family doesn't ____ that company, because it underpays its workers. **(patronize)**

- A ____ of celebrities attended the fundraiser for the animal rescue league. **(galaxy)**

- Do you have the ____ to stand up to a bully? **(nerve)**

3 Read each sentence and ask students to tell which word or words are wrong. Then have them provide the correct word from the week's list.

- Do you have the cowardice to fight a formidable enemy? **(cowardice/nerve)**

- Powerless people persuaded the president to enforce civil rights laws. **(Powerless/Influential)**

- TV and radio ads attempt to persuade shoppers to avoid certain businesses. **(avoid/patronize)**

- The solar system contains many stars and planets. **(solar system/galaxy)**

4 Read each sentence and ask students to decide if it is true or false. If the sentence is false, instruct students to explain why.

- A galaxy is a single star. **(false; it is a system of stars)**

- When you patronize a restaurant, you eat there. **(true)**

- Your nerves carry blood to your heart. **(false; your nerves carry messages to your brain)**

- *Influential* and *powerful* are synonyms. **(true)**

Answers for page 127: 1. C, 2. F, 3. C, 4. G

Name _____

Review Words   nerve • influential • patronize • galaxy

Fill in the bubble next to the correct answer.

1. **Which word is an antonym for *influential*?**
   - Ⓐ harmful
   - Ⓑ persuasive
   - Ⓒ powerless
   - Ⓓ helpful

2. **Which word is an antonym for *nerve*?**
   - Ⓕ cowardice
   - Ⓖ courage
   - Ⓗ intelligence
   - Ⓙ stupidity

3. **Which sentence does not use the word *galaxy* correctly?**
   - Ⓐ One day, traveling to a far-off galaxy may be commonplace.
   - Ⓑ A galaxy of fabulous musicians will be featured at the festival.
   - Ⓒ A galaxy of chattering first-graders waited at the bus stop.
   - Ⓓ The Andromeda Galaxy is a spiral nebula, as is the Milky Way.

4. **Which is true of someone who *patronizes* a store?**
   - Ⓕ He or she owns it.
   - Ⓖ He or she shops there.
   - Ⓗ He or she refuses to shop there.
   - Ⓙ He or she advertises its products.

Writing

Write about why you like to patronize a particular store or restaurant. Use **patronize** in your sentences.

_____

_____

_____

courteous

adjective

polite

antonym:
disrespectful

My parents expect me to be **courteous** and to use good manners when I speak to adults.

Which words mean about the same as **courteous**?

- rude
- rough
- unkind
- thoughtful
- considerate

What are some things you might say that would be **courteous**?

burrow

verb

to dig a hole in the ground

Rodents such as moles and groundhogs make tunnels by **burrowing** underground.

Complete this graphic organizer for **burrow**.

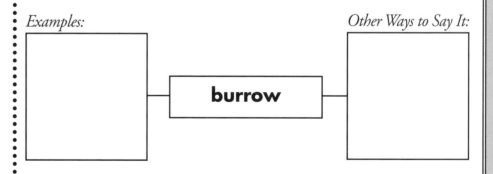

Examples:

burrow

Other Ways to Say It:

What other types of animals **burrow** in the ground?

intuition

noun

the ability to guess about something correctly

My **intuition** was right! There is a surprise quiz today.

Which words have about the same meaning as **intuition**?

- logic
- instinct
- insight
- intelligence
- hunch

Has your **intuition** ever given you a feeling that something was about to happen? Were you right? What happened?

gorgeous

adjective

very pleasing to look at

synonym: dazzling

The tropical garden was filled with **gorgeous** plants and birds.

Which words mean about the same as **gorgeous**?

- grand
- lovely
- hideous
- stunning
- unattractive

What is something in nature that you think is **gorgeous**?

courteous • burrow • intuition • gorgeous

Write on the board the four words studied this week. Read the words with the class and briefly review their meanings. Then conduct the oral activities below.

1 Tell students that you are going to give them a clue about one of the words for the week. They are to find the word that answers the clue.

- You might use this word to describe a beautiful view. (**gorgeous**)

- This word describes people with excellent manners. (**courteous**)

- Gophers and rabbits do this. (**burrow in the ground**)

- You might use this to help you decide whether you can trust someone. (**your intuition**)

2 Read each sentence and ask students to supply the correct word to complete the sentence.

- Soldiers often use their ____ to avoid danger. (**intuition**)

- Rabbits ____ in the ground, creating safe places to care for their babies. (**burrow**)

- If you were more ____ to others, they would probably treat you more politely. (**courteous**)

- Wow! Just look at the brilliant colors in that ____ sunset. (**gorgeous**)

3 Read each sentence and ask students to tell which word or words are wrong. Then have them provide the correct word from the week's list.

- "Pardon me?" is a rude way to ask "What did you say?" (**rude/courteous**)

- You must be so proud of your unattractive rose garden! (**unattractive/gorgeous**)

- Tunneling creatures such as gophers launch into the ground. (**launch/burrow**)

- I trust my direct knowledge to tell me if someone is speaking the truth. (**direct knowledge/intuition**)

4 Read each sentence and ask students to decide if it is true or false. If the sentence is false, instruct students to explain why.

- Intuition helps people to make guesses and decisions. (**true**)

- It's courteous to interrupt people when they're speaking. (**false; it's rude**)

- Giraffes burrow in the ground. (**false; their bodies are ill-suited for it**)

- *Gorgeous* and *spectacular* are synonyms. (**true**)

Answers for page 131: 1. D, 2. G, 3. B, 4. F

Review Words courteous • burrow • intuition • gorgeous

Fill in the bubble next to the correct answer.

1. **Which word is an antonym for *gorgeous*?**
   Ⓐ minuscule
   Ⓑ massive
   Ⓒ beautiful
   Ⓓ hideous

2. **Which word is an antonym for *courteous*?**
   Ⓕ cowardly
   Ⓖ disrespectful
   Ⓗ polite
   Ⓙ daring

3. **When might someone need *intuition*?**
   Ⓐ when he or she is adding 12 and 6
   Ⓑ when he or she is solving a mystery
   Ⓒ when he or she is washing dishes
   Ⓓ when he or she is eating breakfast

4. **In which sentence could *burrow* be used to fill in the blank?**
   Ⓕ My cat likes to ____ under the covers and sleep beside my feet.
   Ⓖ My sister lets me ____ her jewelry and purses once in a while.
   Ⓗ ____ is another word for dresser or chest of drawers.
   Ⓙ Donkeys are sturdy animals that can carry a heavy ____.

Writing

Write to describe the most gorgeous sight you've ever seen. Use **gorgeous** in your sentences.

_____

_____

_____

integrate

verb

1. to bring together into a whole

2. to make open to all races of people

The school board will **integrate** many people's ideas in developing a plan to **integrate** all of the schools in our district.

Which meaning is being used: "to open to all people" or "to unite into a whole"?

- The class wrote a story that integrated everyone's ideas.
- Her decor successfully integrates old and new furniture.
- The golf club was integrated in the 1980s when non-white members were first welcomed.
- Jackie Robinson was the first black player on an integrated major league team.
- Fusion cooking integrates the ingredients of several cultures.

What book have you read that **integrates** more than one genre, such as mystery and humor?

priority

noun

the most important thing at a certain time

My highest **priority** after school is to get my homework done. Then I can enjoy leisure activities.

Complete this graphic organizer for **priority**.

Examples: *Other Ways to Say It:*

priority

What is your highest **priority** in today's schedule? What about for this weekend?

customary

adjective

commonly practiced

In Japan, it is **customary** to remove your shoes when you enter a house.

Which words mean about the same as **customary**?

- uncommon
- traditional
- strange
- routine
- usual

What is something that is **customary** in your home?

lobby

verb

to try to convince others, especially lawmakers, to decide in your favor

noun

a hall or room at the entrance to a building

Nature lovers have had to **lobby** the government to protect redwood forests. The **lobby** of the state capitol was filled with protestors.

Which definition is being used: "to try to convince lawmakers" or "a room at the entrance"?

- I waited in the hotel lobby for the taxi to arrive.
- Animal rights groups lobby for laws protecting animals.
- Groups of workers often lobby for an increase in wages.
- Mom scolded us for playing tag in the bank lobby.
- Our lobby to reduce nightly homework fell on deaf ears.

What do you feel strongly enough about that you would **lobby** your government representatives?

integrate • priority • customary • lobby

Write on the board the four words studied this week. Read the words with the class and briefly review their meanings. Then conduct the oral activities below.

1 Tell students that you are going to give them a clue about one of the words for the week. They are to find the word that answers the clue.

- A hotel has one. (**a lobby**)

- This word describes people's usual routines. (**customary**)

- A firefighter's highest one is to save lives. (**priority**)

- In the mid-1900s, lawmakers and courts began to do this to U.S. schools. (**integrate them**)

2 Read each sentence and ask students to supply the correct word to complete the sentence.

- It's ___ for students to eat lunch together. (**customary**)

- This recipe successfully ___ Asian and Italian flavors. (**integrates**)

- In efforts to protect people's constitutional rights, civil rights groups often ___ lawmakers. (**lobby**)

- On weekends, my highest ___ is to relax and have fun. (**priority**)

3 Read each sentence and ask students to tell which word or words are wrong. Then have them provide the correct word from the week's list.

- To segregate restaurants, Congress made it unlawful to exclude people because of their race. (**segregate/integrate**)

- In the U.S., it's unusual to eat with a knife and fork. (**unusual/customary**)

- Hotel guests step through the front door and into the kitchen. (**kitchen/lobby**)

- This important job takes last place over all others. (**last place/priority**)

4 Read each sentence and ask students to decide if it is true or false. If the sentence is false, instruct students to explain why.

- Chatting with friends should be a good student's top priority. (**false; learning should be top priority**)

- *Lobby* and *entryway* are synonyms. (**true**)

- In the latter part of the 20th century, civil rights protesters in the U.S. struggled to integrate businesses and public institutions. (**true**)

- *Customary* and *traditional* are synonyms. (**true**)

Answers for page 135: 1. C, 2. J, 3. B, 4. F

Review Words   integrate • priority • customary • lobby

Fill in the bubble next to the correct answer.

1. **Which word is an antonym for *customary*?**
   Ⓐ rude
   Ⓑ courteous
   Ⓒ uncommon
   Ⓓ usual

2. **Which word is an antonym for *integrate*?**
   Ⓕ lessen
   Ⓖ double
   Ⓗ combine
   Ⓙ segregate

3. **Which should be a driver's highest *priority*?**
   Ⓐ to find a parking lot
   Ⓑ to drive safely
   Ⓒ to drive at top speeds
   Ⓓ to drive at low speeds

4. **Which sentence could not be completed with the word *lobby*?**
   Ⓕ Horseback riding is a time-consuming and expensive ____.
   Ⓖ Auto insurance companies are likely to ____ for a hands-free cellphone law.
   Ⓗ When you reach the ground floor, the elevator opens to the ____.
   Ⓙ The floor of the ____ was covered with fine marble.

Writing

Write about what you think will be one priority in your life when you are an adult.
Use **priority** in your sentences.

_____

_____

_____

charade

noun

1. a game in which someone acts out a phrase, using gestures and no words (usually plural)

2. an obviously insincere action

When we play **charades**, my friend Leo pretends to have fun, but I can tell his enthusiasm is a **charade**.

Which meaning is being referenced: "a game of pantomime" or "an insincere action"?

- use hands to impart a phrase
- gesture to give clues
- fake it
- not really mean it
- guess what someone is acting out

When you play **charades**, do you like to be the actor or one of the guessers?

jovial

adjective

full of fun

Our coach is so **jovial** that even strenuous workouts are fun.

Complete this graphic organizer for **jovial**.

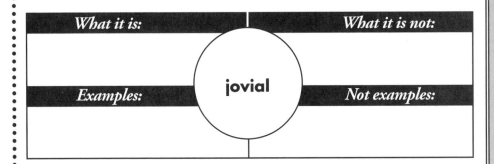

What it is:		What it is not:
	jovial	
Examples:		Not examples:

Who is the most **jovial** person you know? How does this person behave?

motto

noun

a short sentence or phrase that expresses a guiding belief

Her positive approach to life is revealed in her **motto**: "Carpe diem—Seize the day!"

Which words mean about the same as **motto**?

- saying
- slogan
- phrase
- diary
- book

Companies and teams often have **mottoes**. Why do you think this is so? Tell some **mottoes** that you know. What is your favorite **motto**?

innovation

noun

something newly introduced

The first automobile was a major **innovation** in transportation.

Which of the following were **innovations** within the last 100 years?

- the Internet
- books
- automobiles
- jumbo passenger jets
- rap music

Give examples of other **innovations** and how they changed our lives.

charade • jovial • motto • innovation

Write on the board the four words studied this week. Read the words with the class and briefly review their meanings. Then conduct the oral activities below.

1 Tell students that you are going to give them a clue about one of the words for the week. They are to find the word that answers the clue.

- In the 1970s, the personal computer was one. (**an innovation**)

- "To protect and to serve" is one that many police departments have. (**a motto**)

- This is a guessing game. (**charades**)

- This word describes someone who loves to laugh. (**jovial**)

2 Read each sentence and ask students to supply the correct word to complete the sentence.

- Our _____ host made everyone laugh by telling hilarious jokes and stories. (**jovial**)

- Since I'm not a very good mime, I lost when we played _____ last night. (**charades**)

- In the 1950s, the transmission of television programs was an _____ in home entertainment. (**innovation**)

- Many companies have a _____ that tells the main purpose of the business. (**motto**)

3 Read each list of words and phrases. Ask students to supply the word that fits best with each.

- belief, saying, guiding principle (**motto**)

- latest style, modernization, invention (**innovation**)

- cheerful, giggly, jolly, fun-loving (**jovial**)

- insincere actions, faking something, pretending something (**charade**)

4 Read each sentence and ask students to decide if it is true or false. If the sentence is false, instruct students to explain why.

- If you take part in a charade, you are pretending to be something you're not. (**true**)

- "Be prepared" is a motto. (**true**)

- A jovial person takes most aspects of life very seriously. (**false; he or she sees the lighter side of things**)

- An innovation is a device or custom that people developed long ago. (**false; it is something that people developed recently**)

Answers for page 139: 1. D, 2. F, 3. B, 4. G

Review Words   charade • jovial • motto • innovation

Fill in the bubble next to the correct answer.

1. **Which word is an antonym for *innovation*?**
   Ⓐ slavery
   Ⓑ freedom
   Ⓒ modernization
   Ⓓ tradition

2. **Which word is an antonym for *jovial*?**
   Ⓕ grumpy
   Ⓖ jolly
   Ⓗ reliable
   Ⓙ carefree

3. **Which is a rule in *charades*?**
   Ⓐ You can't gesture.
   Ⓑ You can't speak.
   Ⓒ The oldest player goes first.
   Ⓓ The youngest player goes first.

4. **Which of these is a *motto*?**
   Ⓕ "Ouch!"
   Ⓖ "Swifter, Higher, Stronger"
   Ⓗ "Congratulations!"
   Ⓙ "Please pass the butter."

Writing

Write about an innovation that you hope will be developed by the year 2030.
Use **innovation** in your sentences.

_____

_____

_____

ramshackle

adjective

ready to collapse

synonym: rickety

We came across a **ramshackle** cabin on our walk in the woods.

Which word or words mean about the same as **ramshackle**?

- in disrepair
- remodeled
- renovated
- run-down
- dilapidated

Describe a **ramshackle** place or object that you've seen.

confident

adjective

having trust or faith

I am **confident** that I can pass this test.

Complete this graphic organizer for **confident**.

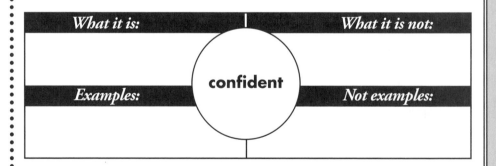

What it is:		*What it is not:*
	confident	
Examples:		*Not examples:*

What is something you feel **confident** about?

honorary

adjective

given or held as an honor and not involving the usual requirements or duties

Famous people often receive **honorary** degrees from universities.

Which of the following could be **honorary**?

- citizenship
- grades
- a club membership
- a team mascot
- a friend

Think of a famous person. What sort of **honorary** degree do you think that person deserves?

literacy

noun

the ability to read and write

Literacy is important for succeeding in our society.

Which of the following activities demonstrate **literacy**?

- reading a sign
- watching a movie
- making a shopping list
- singing a popular song
- sending an e-mail message

Give some reasons why **literacy** is important.

ramshackle • confident • honorary • literacy

Write on the board the four words studied this week. Read the words with the class and briefly review their meanings. Then conduct the oral activities below.

1 Tell students that you are going to give them a clue about one of the words for the week. They are to find the word that answers the clue.

- Without this, you can't read street signs. **(literacy)**

- This word describes someone who feels sure that he or she can do something. **(confident)**

- This word describes a treehouse that's about to collapse. **(ramshackle)**

- This word describes an award that a person has not necessarily fulfilled the requirements for. **(honorary)**

2 Read each sentence and ask students to supply the correct word to complete the sentence.

- At the public library, ____ volunteers teach adults to read and write. **(literacy)**

- Do you feel ____ about the race, or are you afraid that you won't win first place? **(confident)**

- A famous author, Ms. Tyler, received an ____ degree from a local university. **(honorary)**

- Who could possibly live in that ____ little shed? **(ramshackle)**

3 Read each sentence and ask students to tell which word or words are wrong. Then have them provide the correct word from the week's list.

- That sturdy old house is unsafe to enter. **(sturdy/ramshackle)**

- Because she baked so many cookies for the Scouts, Mrs. Smith was made a temporary member of the troop. **(a temporary/an honorary)**

- Annabelle is worried that she will win next week's election. **(worried/confident)**

4 Read each sentence and ask students to decide if it is true or false. If the sentence is false, instruct students to explain why.

- You shouldn't enter a ramshackle building. **(true)**

- Most recipients feel ashamed of honorary titles. **(false; most recipients are proud of them)**

- *Confident* and *sure* are synonyms. **(true)**

- Today, most societies highly value literacy. **(true)**

Answers for page 143: 1. D, 2. H, 3. C, 4. G

Review Words   ramshackle • confident • honorary • literacy

Fill in the bubble next to the correct answer.

1. **Which word is an antonym for *confident*?**
   Ⓐ ungrateful
   Ⓑ inconsiderate
   Ⓒ unconscious
   Ⓓ uncertain

2. **Which word is an antonym for *ramshackle*?**
   Ⓕ modern
   Ⓖ ancient
   Ⓗ sturdy
   Ⓙ rickety

3. **To whom is a college most likely to give *honorary* degrees?**
   Ⓐ students who attend that college for four years
   Ⓑ instructors who have just started teaching college
   Ⓒ people who are famous for important achievements
   Ⓓ high school students who have applied for admission

4. ***Literacy* is the ability to _____.**
   Ⓕ sing and dance
   Ⓖ read and write
   Ⓗ add and subtract
   Ⓙ earn lots of money

Writing

Write about how your life might be different if you couldn't read or write. Use **literacy** in your sentences.

_____

_____

_____

overcast

adjective

covered with clouds

I wanted to dry the clothes in the sun, but the sky was **overcast**.

Which words might describe an **overcast** day?

- gloomy
- dark
- bright
- dreary
- dull

Name some activities that are not easily done on an **overcast** day. Name some activities that you can do on an **overcast** day.

slovenly

adjective

untidy in dress or appearance

When I returned from camping, I looked a little **slovenly**.

Complete this graphic organizer for **slovenly**.

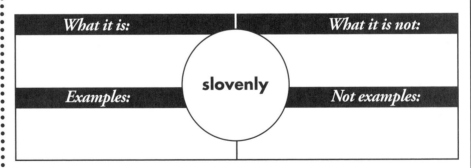

Why might someone look **slovenly**? Do you ever look **slovenly**? When?

tirade

noun

a long, angry speech

The coach's pre-game **tirade** did not help to encourage the team.

Which of the following are likely to give a **tirade** from time to time?

- a baby
- a judge
- a teacher
- a teenager
- a military commander

Have you ever had to listen to a **tirade**? Who gave it? What was it about?

oblivious

adjective

not being aware or not paying attention

My older sister is always running into things because she is **oblivious** to her surroundings.

Which words mean about the same as **oblivious**?

- unaware
- mindful
- inattentive
- ignorant
- unconscious

Tell about something that happened to you at a time you were **oblivious**.

overcast • slovenly • tirade • oblivious

Write on the board the four words studied this week. Read the words with the class and briefly review their meanings. Then conduct the oral activities below.

1 Tell students that you are going to give them a clue about one of the words for the week. They are to find the word that answers the clue.

- If drivers are this way, they may cause traffic accidents. (**oblivious**)

- This word describes someone who's dressed in, sloppy, dirty clothes. (**slovenly**)

- This word probably describes the sky during a heavy rain. (**overcast**)

- This is the opposite of a short, humorous speech. (**a tirade**)

2 Read each sentence and ask students to supply the correct word to complete the sentence.

- Once in a while, Mom launches into a _____ about the condition of my room. (**tirade**)

- He seems to be _____ that his shoes are always untied. (**oblivious**)

- Along the coast, fog can cause the sky to be _____. (**overcast**)

- He's a nice guy, but his _____ appearance puts people off. (**slovenly**)

3 Read each sentence and ask students to tell which word or words are wrong. Then have them provide the correct word from the week's list.

- If it's sunny again tomorrow, I think we should cancel our picnic. (**sunny/overcast**)

- After our teacher's celebratory speech on rude behavior, we all tried to behave more politely. (**celebratory speech/tirade**)

- The boys looked clean and tidy in their grimy, ill-fitting clothes. (**clean and tidy/slovenly**)

- You must be attentive to not have seen that huge puddle you just stepped in. (**attentive/oblivious**)

4 Read each sentence and ask students to decide if it is true or false. If the sentence is false, instruct students to explain why.

- A person who is not aware of what's going on is oblivious. (**true**)

- Tirades are happy expressions. (**false; tirades express anger**)

- *Overcast* and *cloudy* are synonyms. (**true**)

- *Slovenly* and *sloppy* are synonyms. (**true**)

Answers for page 147: 1. C, 2. F, 3. B, 4. G

Name _____

Fill in the bubble next to the correct answer.

1. **Which word is an antonym for *slovenly*?**
   - Ⓐ messy
   - Ⓑ cranky
   - Ⓒ tidy
   - Ⓓ jolly

2. **Which word is an antonym for *oblivious*?**
   - Ⓕ mindful
   - Ⓖ gleeful
   - Ⓗ ignorant
   - Ⓙ unknowing

3. **Which is the most likely topic for a teacher's *tirade*?**
   - Ⓐ graduating students' achievements
   - Ⓑ students' low scores on the last math test
   - Ⓒ a fascinating article in today's newspaper
   - Ⓓ the cute things that her new puppy does

4. **In which sentence could *overcast* be used to fill in the blank?**
   - Ⓕ This street crosses the highway by means of an ____.
   - Ⓖ Along the coast, it is ____ in the morning and then sunny in the afternoon.
   - Ⓗ The front edges of a shirt ____ each other.
   - Ⓙ That book wasn't very interesting. I think it was ____ by other students.

Writing

Write about when it is all right to appear slovenly and when it isn't all right.
Use **slovenly** in your sentences.

_____

_____

_____

Dictionary

Aa

absorb • *verb*

1. to involve or engage completely
2. to take in or soak up

Marta is absorbed by an interest in horses. She absorbs all the books she can find on the subject.

adaptation • *noun*

something that has been changed to fit different conditions

The movie version of The Lion, the Witch and the Wardrobe *was an excellent adaptation of the book.*

akimbo • *adjective*

with hands on hips and elbows turned outward

When my mother stands with her arms akimbo, I know she means business.

ambiguous • *adjective*

having more than one possible meaning

synonym: vague

The judge asked the witness to clarify her ambiguous answer.

amuse • *verb*

1. to entertain
2. to cause to smile or laugh

The boys read comic books to amuse themselves during the long cross-country flight. The antics of the comic-book characters amused them.

ancient • *adjective*

from times long past

The ancient pyramids of Egypt still stand today.

anonymous • *adjective*

from someone whose name is not known

The ancient Greek poem is by an anonymous author.

antique • *noun*

something made a long time ago

Our dining room table, which we inherited from my great-grandmother, is an antique.

aquatic • *adjective*

in water or taking place in water

The aquatic plants lent a lush look to our fish tank.

array • *noun*

1. a large or impressive group or display
2. beautiful or splendid clothing

An array of brightly colored flowers lined the parade route. Soon, the queen appeared in royal array.

authentic • *adjective*

the real thing

antonym: imitation

This store sells authentic Native American jewelry and baskets.

avert • *verb*

1. to turn away from
2. to prevent

A sudden noise made the driver avert his eyes from the road for an instant. Fortunately, he was able to avert an accident by refocusing on the traffic ahead.

Bb

ballyhoo • *noun*

a noisy disturbance; an uproar

There was a big ballyhoo as the home team took the field.

banish • verb

to punish someone by making him or her permanently leave a country

The king banished the knight for betraying his master.

banter • noun

playful, teasing conversation

synonym: repartee

At the end of each newscast, the news anchor and the sportscaster like to engage in banter about the local baseball team's performance.

benefactor • noun

someone who gives generous assistance or a gift of money

Mr. Lawson was one of the major benefactors for the new community swimming pool.

bountiful • adjective

more than enough

synonym: plenty

Because everyone brought something to eat, we had a bountiful amount of food for the potluck.

buoyant • adjective

1. capable of floating
2. having a lighthearted, cheerful nature

The inner tube was buoyant enough to support three people.

burrow • verb

to dig a hole in the ground

Rodents such as moles and groundhogs make tunnels by burrowing underground.

Cc

calligraphy • noun

a style of beautiful or elegant handwriting

The invitations were painstakingly hand-lettered in elegant calligraphy.

campaign • noun

a series of planned activities to bring about a desired result

The women's club staged a campaign to convince the city council to refurbish the homeless shelter.

cavort • verb

to run and jump around playfully

The children love to cavort in the sprinklers on hot afternoons.

charade • noun

1. a game in which someone acts out a phrase, using gestures and no words (usually plural)
2. an obviously insincere action

When we play charades, my friend Leo pretends to have fun, but I can tell his enthusiasm is a charade.

charisma • noun

an unusual ability to influence people and inspire devotion

Kali's charisma made her a popular choice for class president.

circumstance • noun

a fact connected with a particular event, such as time, location, and other specifics

The heat and lack of air conditioning made for very difficult test-taking circumstances.

compel • *verb*

to force to some action

The student's mischievous behavior throughout the assembly compelled the principal to send him to the office.

compose • *verb*

1. to become calm
2. to create by putting together words or musical notes

The pianist took a moment to compose himself before he stepped onstage to perform the music he had composed.

comprehend • *verb*

to understand

A good teacher can help you comprehend even difficult math problems.

concise • *adjective*

expressed in a few words

synonym: brief

Isaac's report was concise yet packed with information.

concoct • *verb*

1. to prepare by mixing several different things together; to combine
2. to make up something untruthful

I love to concoct smoothies with frozen fruit, yogurt, and juice.

confident • *adjective*

having trust or faith

I am confident that I can pass this test.

conform • *verb*

to act or think in a way that follows the rules

I'd rather sit on the floor, but in school I must conform and sit at a desk.

confront • *verb*

to meet or face boldly

I decided to confront my brother about using my bike without permission.

contemplate • *verb*

to think about for a long time

Jeremy took some time to contemplate the question before he answered it.

converge • *verb*

to come together

synonym: to merge

Main Street and Elm Street converge at the center of town.

courteous • *adjective*

polite

antonym: disrespectful

My parents expect me to be courteous and to use good manners when I speak to adults.

customary • *adjective*

commonly practiced

In Japan, it is customary to remove your shoes when you enter a house.

Dd

deception • *noun*

a trick or lie meant to deceive someone

The movie villain's deception to disguise his identity was uncovered by the clever detective.

dedicate • *verb*

to set apart for a special purpose or use

synonym: devote

We will dedicate the new building for use as a computer lab.

descend • *verb*

to move from a higher place to a lower place

The squirrel quickly descended from the treetop to the ground.

detest • *verb*

to dislike very much

I know that spinach has lots of iron and is a healthy food, but I still detest it.

digit • *noun*

1. a numeral
2. a finger or toe

How many digits are in the number one million? Do you have enough digits to represent all those zeros?

dignity • *noun*

a manner or quality that makes a person worthy of respect

Even though the actor momentarily forgot his lines, he managed to pick up and continue with dignity.

diplomatic • *adjective*

skillful at dealing with people

My teacher is so diplomatic at giving feedback that I never get my feelings hurt when she corrects me.

distraction • *noun*

something that draws one's attention to it

The backyard party next door was a big distraction as I tried to concentrate on my homework.

Ee

encumber • *verb*

to weigh down or burden

The escaping robber was encumbered by the heavy sack of loot.

endeavor

noun

a serious attempt to do something

verb

to make an effort

He was successful in his endeavor to get A's in his science classes. His plan is to endeavor to become a scientist.

endorse • *verb*

1. to give support or approval to
2. to sign one's name

Famous athletes sometimes endorse athletic gear. They have to endorse a contract to make a legal agreement with a sporting gear company.

endow • *verb*

1. to provide with an ability, talent, or other positive qualities at birth
2. to give money or property to

The scientist was endowed with an astounding ability to invent new technologies. With his fortune, he has endowed science programs in many schools.

enlist • *verb*

1. to get the help or support of
2. to join the armed forces

Can we enlist your help in collecting cellphones? We want to send them to soldiers who enlist in the army and are sent overseas.

enthrall • *verb*

to hold one's interest completely

synonym: to entrance

I was enthralled by the book and read nonstop for hours.

enunciate • *verb*

to pronounce words, especially in a clear voice

Our teacher enunciates so that students who are learning English can understand her.

erroneous • *adjective*

containing an error

antonym: correct

The garage sale address given in the newspaper was erroneous, so we never found the right location.

esophagus • *noun*

the tube that carries food from the throat to the stomach

The human esophagus is about nine inches long.

essential • *adjective*

very important or necessary

Sugar is an essential ingredient in making sugar cookies.

esteem • *noun*

a very positive opinion

synonym: respect

Anita was held in high esteem because of all her volunteer work in the community.

exaggerate • *verb*

to make something seem larger, more important, or more valuable than it actually is

Tall tales usually exaggerate and attribute superhuman traits to the characters.

expose • *verb*

1. to make something known
2. to leave without protection

The detective exposed the professor as the mastermind of the plot. The invisible ink appeared when it was exposed to sunlight.

extricate • *verb*

to set free from a difficult or embarrassing situation

antonym: to trap

The bear struggled to extricate itself from the net.

Ff

familiar • *adjective*

1. well-known; easily recognized
2. knowing something or someone well

I am very familiar with this book because I read it last year. Its theme, the challenges of growing up, is a familiar one.

fastidious • *adjective*

not easy to please

The fastidious eater complained about every dish at dinner.

fatigue • *noun*

the condition of being very tired

synonym: exhaustion

I felt extreme fatigue after the twenty-mile bike ride.

fiasco • *noun*

a complete failure

The pool party was a fiasco due to the lightning storm.

finance

noun

affairs related to money

verb

to provide money for someone or something

My mother has been very successful in finance. The profits from her investments helped finance our family's restaurant.

flaunt • *verb*

to display noticeably

My cousin loves to flaunt her expensive clothes whenever she has a chance.

forfeit • *verb*

to give up the right to something

We had to forfeit the soccer game because we did not have enough players.

formidable • *adjective*

exceptionally difficult or fearsome

The heavyweight boxer had not lost a bout and was considered a formidable opponent.

frontier • *noun*

the farthest reaches of settlement, exploration, or knowledge

There are few geographic frontiers remaining on Earth, but science has many new frontiers to explore.

Gg

galaxy • *noun*

1. a group of brilliant, beautiful, or famous people
2. a large group of stars and planets, and other matter

A galaxy of notable astronomers gathered to discuss the recent photographs of the Andromeda Galaxy.

gesture

noun

a movement of the hands or head that has meaning

verb

to move your hands or head to emphasize what you are saying or thinking

An international gesture meaning "silence" is an index finger pressed to the lips. People from some cultures gesture more than others when they speak.

glare

verb

to stare in an angry way

noun

a strong, bright light

The driver glared at us when my mom pulled out in front of him. She didn't see him because of the glare on the windshield.

gorgeous • *adjective*

very pleasing to look at

synonym: dazzling

The tropical garden was filled with gorgeous plants and birds.

gritty • *adjective*

feeling like sand

After the dentist drilled my tooth, I felt something gritty in my mouth.

Hh

honorary • *adjective*

given or held as an honor and not involving the usual requirements or duties

Famous people often receive honorary degrees from universities.

Ii

idle • *adjective*

not busy; doing nothing

synonym: lazy

I like to spend my idle hours on a rainy day watching old movies.

ignorance • *noun*

a lack of knowledge

I decided to overcome my ignorance of computer programming and take a class.

immobile • *adjective*

unable to move

synonym: motionless

A car is totally immobile without its battery.

indispensable • *adjective*

absolutely necessary

Although we can live a long time without food, water is indispensable.

infinite • *adjective*

without limits; without end

The universe contains an infinite number of stars.

influential • *adjective*

being able to change or affect someone or something

A very influential music teacher convinced me to continue studying the cello.

innovation • *noun*

something newly introduced

The first automobile was a major innovation in transportation.

integrate • *verb*

1. to bring together into a whole
2. to make open to all races of people

The school board will integrate many people's ideas in developing a plan to integrate all of the schools in our district.

intimate • *adjective*

close and familiar

My mother has been intimate friends with Mrs. Mendez since they were in high school.

intuition • *noun*

the ability to guess about something correctly

My intuition was right! There is a surprise quiz today.

irresistible • *adjective*

impossible to resist

The fuzzy stuffed dog was so irresistible that I just had to buy it.

Jj

jester • *noun*

someone who always jokes or acts playfully

Always the jester, Billy showed up for the field trip wearing his sister's bunny slippers.

jovial • *adjective*

full of fun

Our coach is so jovial that even strenuous workouts are fun.

jubilant • *adjective*

feeling or showing great joy

synonym: ecstatic

The streets were filled with jubilant spectators as the Olympic victors paraded past.

juvenile • *adjective*

1. not mature; young
2. immature in actions; childish

The marathon organizer gave a special prize for juvenile runners.

Kk

know-how • *noun*

the knowledge of how to do something

A carpenter has real know-how when it comes to building things.

Ll

limber • *adjective*

bending easily

synonym: flexible

Gymnasts must be strong and limber to do all those flips and jumps.

literacy • *noun*

the ability to read and write

Literacy is important for succeeding in our society.

lobby

verb

to try to convince others, especially lawmakers, to decide in your favor

noun

a hall or room at the entrance to a building

Nature lovers have had to lobby the government to protect redwood forests. The lobby of the state capitol was filled with protestors.

lunge • *verb*

to move forward suddenly

The kitten lunged at my fish sandwich.

luscious • *adjective*

smelling or tasting delicious

The peach pie with vanilla ice cream was a luscious dessert.

Mm

majestic • *adjective*

grand or spectacular

antonym: inferior

As we left the lowlands, majestic, snowcapped mountains rose up in the distance.

majority • *noun*

more than half or most of something

The majority of the students in my class ride a bus to school. The majority opinion is that riding the bus is fun.

mesmerize • *verb*

to fascinate

synonym: to entrance

The meteor shower mesmerized everyone who saw it.

mischievous • *adjective*

playful and mildly naughty

The mischievous puppy chewed on all my shoes.

moderate • *adjective*

not too much or too little

Moderate amounts of dark chocolate have health benefits, but don't overdo it.

mortify • *verb*

to cause someone to feel terrible embarrassment

At my graduation party, my brother mortified me when he began to sing off-key into the karaoke machine.

motto • *noun*

a short sentence or phrase that expresses a guiding belief

Her positive approach to life is revealed in her motto: "Carpe diem—Seize the day!"

murmur • *verb*

to say words in a soft voice

It's OK to talk in the library if you murmur.

Nn

nerve • *noun*

1. a bundle of fibers connecting the brain and parts of the body
2. courage or bravery

Every nerve in my body was on edge until the firefighter came out safely. He had a lot of nerve to run into the burning building.

Oo

oblivious • *adjective*

not being aware or not paying attention

My older sister is always running into things because she is oblivious to her surroundings.

obsolete • *adjective*

no longer in use

Just as CDs made records a thing of the past, DVDs made videocassettes obsolete.

overcast • *adjective*

covered with clouds

I wanted to dry the clothes in the sun, but the sky was overcast.

Pp

patronize • *verb*

to regularly shop at or use the services of
synonym: to frequent

My parents prefer to patronize the locally owned market instead of the national chain.

perennial • *adjective*

lasting through the year or for many years
synonym: constant

Perennial flowers, such as roses and irises, are sure to bloom again next year.

persistent • *adjective*

1. not giving up
2. lasting a long time

The persistent hikers finally overcame the last obstacle and reached the summit. Their ordeal left them with persistent aches and pains.

pessimistic • *adjective*

expecting things to turn out badly
antonym: optimistic

Andrea is so pessimistic! She is sure that it will rain on the day of the class picnic.

petty • *adjective*

not important

When we divided the lunch bill, it seemed petty to argue over who would pay the extra five cents.

pharmacist • *noun*

a person trained to prepare and give out medicines

The pharmacist filled my prescription and made sure I understood the instructions for taking the medication.

priority • *noun*

the most important thing at a certain time

My highest priority after school is to get my homework done. Then I can enjoy leisure activities.

promotion • *noun*

a move upward in position or grade

My mother's promotion at work meant that we could afford music lessons.

pucker • *verb*

to gather or contract into folds or wrinkles

Your lips might pucker when you taste a lemon.

Qq

queue • *noun*

a line formed for waiting

The queue to buy tickets wrapped all around the theater and extended into the parking lot.

quizzical • *adjective*

expressing doubt or questioning; puzzled

Mom looked quizzical when she received a birthday card from someone whose name she didn't recognize.

Rr

ramshackle • *adjective*

ready to collapse

synonym: rickety

We came across a ramshackle cabin on our walk in the woods.

reluctant • *adjective*

unwilling

The young boy was reluctant to jump into the deep end of the pool.

repose • *noun*

freedom from activity or responsibility

After a long week at school, I find repose in lounging on the couch, watching cartoons.

restoration • *noun*

the act of bringing something back to its original condition

The restoration of the old house took more than a year.

reunion • *noun*

the bringing together of friends, family, or other groups of people

Family members from all across the country got together at our reunion.

Ss

sanction • *verb*

to give approval

The school board sanctioned the building of a new middle school.

sarcastic • *adjective*

using cutting or bitter words for the purpose of making fun of someone or something

I was already embarrassed about my bad haircut, and my classmates' sarcastic remarks didn't make me feel any better.

sensitive • *adjective*

physically or emotionally responsive

Because Felix is so sensitive to pollen, we need to be sensitive about bringing flowers into the house.

shallow • *adjective*

lacking deep thought, feeling, or knowledge

His shallow remarks about the book exposed his shallow understanding of the author's purpose.

slovenly • *adjective*

untidy in dress or appearance

When I returned from camping, I looked a little slovenly.

stratosphere • *noun*

the layer of atmosphere that extends from about 11 miles to 30 miles above Earth

The stratosphere contains the ozone layer, which absorbs solar radiation, helping the temperatures in the stratosphere to remain fairly constant.

Tt

taunt • *verb*

to tease or make fun of

synonym: mock

The zookeeper had to reprimand some teenagers who were taunting the lion by poking sticks through the bars of its cage.

tendency • *noun*

a likelihood of behaving in a certain way

A puppy has a tendency to chew on things.

terminology • *noun*

the special vocabulary used in a particular business, science, or art

synonym: lingo

Words like byte, software, *and* operating system *are examples of computer terminology.*

tirade • *noun*

a long, angry speech

The coach's pre-game tirade did not help to encourage the team.

tolerant • *adjective*

willing to respect people who think or act differently than you

To have a harmonious classroom, we all need to recognize and be tolerant of our differences.

triumph • *verb*

to obtain a great success or victory

The gymnast triumphed in the competition and won an Olympic gold medal.

Uu

ultimate • *adjective*

final

synonym: last

When the bus reached its ultimate destination, only two passengers remained.

urban • *adjective*

something that is from the city or related to a city

High-rise buildings and taxis are common in urban areas.

utter • *verb*

to make an audible sound with your voice

We tried not to utter a sound as we watched the deer and her fawn walk through our backyard.

Vv

vain • *adjective*

overly proud of one's looks, abilities, or accomplishments

antonym: humble

The vain actor kept photos of himself all over the house.

vehement • *adjective*

expressing strong feelings

synonym: intense

She was vehement about finishing the project by herself.

ventilation • *noun*

the circulation of air

The cabin was hot and stuffy because there was no ventilation.

venture • *noun*

a risky or uncertain undertaking

The business venture turned out to be a financial disaster.

volunteer • *noun*

a person who chooses to work without being paid

The Red Cross counts on many volunteers to help out during natural disasters.

Ww

whim • *noun*

a sudden idea to do something

I'd planned to clean out my closet today, but on a whim, I decided to go roller-skating.

Examples:

Other Ways to Say It:

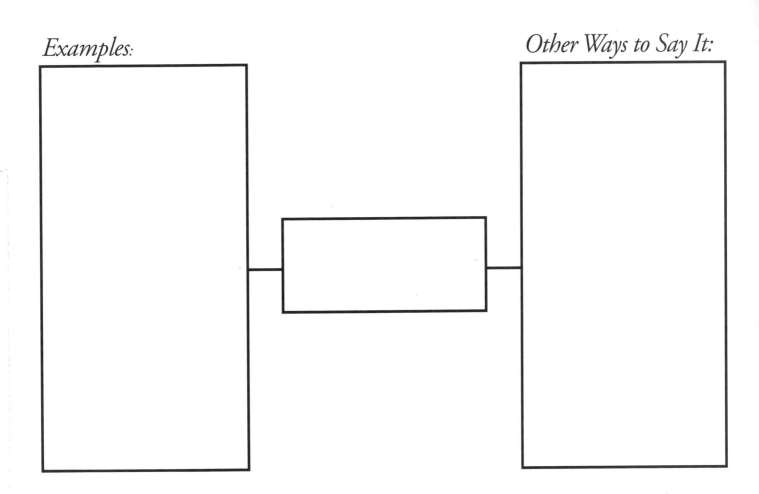

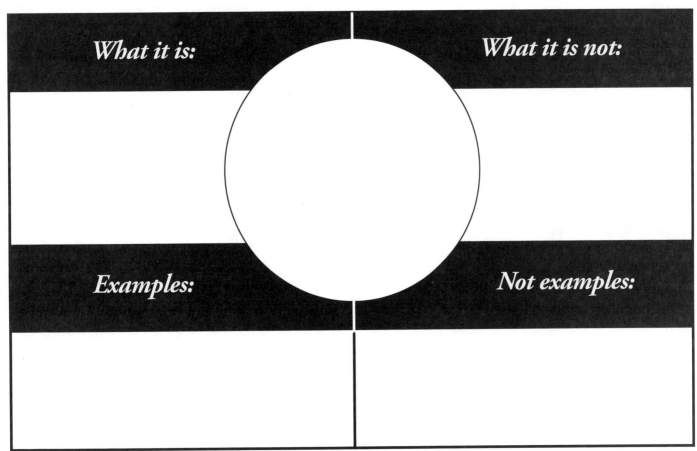

What it is:

What it is not:

Examples:

Not examples:

Index

absorb 45
adaptation 57
akimbo 92
ambiguous 36
amuse 65
ancient 81
anonymous 77
antique 52
aquatic 109
array 32
authentic 121
avert 28
ballyhoo 104
banish 92
banter 108
benefactor 37
bountiful 41
buoyant 113
burrow 128
calligraphy 93
campaign 100
cavort 61
charade 136
charisma 81
circumstance . . . 117
compel 120
compose 69
comprehend 24
concise 108
concoct 101
confident 140
conform 53
confront 33
contemplate 9
converge 60
courteous 128

customary 133
deception 25
dedicate 68
descend 45
detest 73
digit 21
dignity 112
diplomatic 12
distraction 84
encumber 37
endeavor 116
endorse 44
endow 80
enlist 121
enthrall 112
enunciate 105
erroneous 48
esophagus 96
essential 93
esteem 61
exaggerate 16
expose 84
extricate 17
familiar 49
fastidious 29
fatigue 53
fiasco 8
finance 41
flaunt 20
forfeit 85
formidable 96
frontier 20
galaxy 125
gesture 109
glare 68
gorgeous 129

gritty 9
honorary 141
idle 44
ignorance 88
immobile 25
indispensable . . . 40
infinite 56
influential 124
innovation 137
integrate 132
intimate 105
intuition 129
irresistible 120
jester 13
jovial 136
jubilant 49
juvenile 117
know-how 77
limber 100
literacy 141
lobby 133
lunge 29
luscious 85
majestic 101
majority 28
mesmerize 48
mischievous 104
moderate 8
mortify 40
motto 137
murmur 113
nerve 124
oblivious 145
obsolete 13
overcast 144
patronize 125

perennial 24
persistent 17
pessimistic 72
petty 4
pharmacist 97
priority 132
promotion 32
pucker 56
queue 65
quizzical 5
ramshackle 140
reluctant 33
repose 52
restoration 64
reunion 89
sanction 97
sarcastic 60
sensitive 36
shallow 89
slovenly 144
stratosphere 80
taunt 12
tendency 16
terminology 21
tirade 145
tolerant 73
triumph 116
ultimate 76
urban 57
utter 69
vain 88
vehement 64
ventilation 76
venture 4
volunteer 72
whim 5